Winemakers *of the*
WILLAMETTE VALLEY

PIONEERING VINTNERS *from* OREGON'S WINE COUNTRY

VIVIAN PERRY & JOHN VINCENT

FOREWORD BY HARRY PETERSON-NEDRY

AMERICAN PALATE

Published by American Palate
A Division of The History Press
Charleston, SC 29403
www.historypress.net

Cover images: Front: Cristom Vineyards. *Courtesy of John D'Anna*; harvesting Pinot noir grapes. *Courtesy of Polara Studio*. Back: Mount Hood from Maysara Winery. *Courtesy of Maysara Winery*; Cristom Vineyards. *Courtesy of John D'Anna*; harvested Pinot noir grapes. *Courtesy of Ponzi Vineyards*; picking grapes at Chehalem. *Courtesy of Chehalem*.

Illustrations by Sarah Schlesinger.

First published 2013

Manufactured in the United States

ISBN 978.1.60949.676.0

Library of Congress CIP data applied for.

Notice: The information in this book is true and complete to the best of our knowledge. It is offered without guarantee on the part of the authors or The History Press. The authors and The History Press disclaim all liability in connection with the use of this book.

In memory of Forrest Klaffke.

CONTENTS

Contents

FOREWORD

This book is about passion—that key ingredient that rewards idealists even when financial rewards aren't there. And yet it takes a perspective that is unique from other books about Oregon winemakers; indeed, it similarly focuses on passionate souls vital to the industry, but of a *current* generation rather than those who began it all, as other books have done. I call these subjects the "Validation Generation" because they are the ones required to validate the worth of what we did earlier. They nod to us by bringing a passion and drive equal to our own to continuing and improving what we began. These are the ones to whom the baton has been passed.

They have the same impetuous, less-than-rational need to be up to your elbows in grapes at harvest, bear crushing debt on your shoulders, play road warrior marketing wines on back roads of New Jersey you never thought were there and pour wine into plastic cups that busy buyers will never go back to taste. A stubborn will to succeed lives with these modern pioneers, as much as it drove David and Diana Lett unpacking bare rooted grape plants, Dick Erath repairing equipment on his kitchen table or David Adelsheim inviting a filmmaker to shoot in his vineyard for a tale about growing together grapes and a smokable, herbal cash crop in the 1970s. The future of our wine community lives with them, whether second-generation passionistas proudly joining a life they had every right to abandon, growing up usually playing second fiddle to wine in one way or another; professionals hired to put rigor and additional insights into wineries, drinking the Koolaid, embracing their job like a lover and many times spinning off brands of their own; or wide-eyed idealists young and old coming into the wine community with no credentials except conviction, being ready to redo what pioneers did three or four decades before, with a slightly easier path laid out before them but with a lot farther to fall if they failed.

This is a book of potential, both realized and anticipated. And that is so perfect.

My face shows up in here, but only to introduce my daughter, who is a stereotypical second-generation winemaker—born in the same year as my first vineyard, Ridgecrest; a scientist, but better trained than her father both academically and on-the-job; and facing an equal but altogether different set of obstacles, such as how to get the old man out of the way.

Others, like Lynn Penner-Ash, are young enough to be second generation but formative enough to be a pioneer, leading a vanguard of younger female winemakers into the harvest fray. Of course, that said, stalwart pioneers like Pat Campbell, Diana Lett and Nancy Ponzi were talented, wit-endowed, gifted tasters and as critical to the Oregon wine community as any of the fuzzy-faced male pioneers sucking it up for photos at a holiday event—you've seen the photos! No one has a better palate than Pat Campbell, no one had more iconic labels crafted than those Ginny Adelsheim executed, no one was a better strategist and vineyard manager in the first wave than Susan Sokol Blosser, no one has a better laugh than Patty Green, and on and on.

I could do an "I remember" excursion of things at this point, like early Steamboat Winemaker Conferences, especially the one where I bared my soul with early highly technical experiments only to be brought down a rung or two when the experimental design rigor was lost and meant less than the final wine quality; or of working early harvests in others' cellars like Amity, Elk Cove and Erath; or speaking of Dick Erath, whom I admire greatly and with whom I have in common two metal hips, each with the ability to set airport security alarms caterwauling, and who gave the advice when I was viticulturally pubescent and asking some basics about grape plants to "go ask the person you *did* buy them from, if you didn't buy them from me."

Or what about Dave Adelsheim, similarly real-world and to the point, in one of the first of a million consultations or collaborations to come, after I asked how best to sell my first vintage's grapes, advising me to use my wife's contacts since she was a wine writer rather than playing independent and idealistic (are you getting a sense of how I was educated in the ways of the world?); or those no longer with us, like the fastest wit and curmudgeon David Lett, *the* real pioneer and defender of land use, and the equally grumpy at times (not one to suffer fools gladly) and entrepreneurial, as well as yet not made for business, Charles Coury, helping catalyze both Oregon wine and micro-brewing industries; or Dick Ponzi, who made a very successful business in both arenas, equally navigating fine Pinot noir as our first "can do no wrong" winemaker of the '80s and '90s and IPAs with Bridgeport before he sold it and then restaurants afterward in both brewery and in wine country, and *still* he's active lobbying the legislature, as we waded forward in the political swamp this spring to do sensible things to make industries hum.

And how about the place where we all were when we finally decided to do AVAs inside the Willamette Valley after several abortive meetings where we decided not to risk potential dissension in our classically collaborative commune of friends; or where we were when we stopped visiting cities begging people to taste our wine and understand our beauty and, instead, dreamed up OPC in the heads of the Pat Dudleys and David Adelsheims, with me there admiring that process of rich teamwork in which you can't remember and don't care which idea was whose, an innovation that Pied Pipered our customers to come to us to understand the magic of Oregon some fourteen years ago; or when wine pioneers sold grape plants to make ends meet; or when there was *no* lending by banks to vineyards and wineries, so you were forced to maintain an outside job like Dr. Joe Campbell did or were forced to invite friends and family to enjoy the dream by investing some money in your dream (I did both for sixteen and twenty years, respectively); or even how we all invited world-traveling young winemakers to join us at least for harvest, with some to stay for a decade or more, becoming a part of our family, and also invited friends just starting to begin their winery inside ours (we've had more than thirty harvest interns just from New Zealand and more than ten wine brands begin in our house).

The good thing about a book like this, which looks at our great Oregon wine experience from different views, is how it fights the staid, chronological stratification that history often becomes. Because even though people, innovations and external influences all come in waves of time, the reality of this industry is more organic than that, more fluid, washing back and forth like the real sea does, to where the water is turbid from issues still unsettled being kicked up and the edges of the waves are blurred with age and experience, neither mattering after a certain point. After a point, only the passion matters.

And Vivian and John have done well to capture that passion and energy in its raw state, giving vignettes of winemakers making new art out of well-worn principles. Enjoy, celebrate and wait for things to change even more, passion being the only constant.

—Harry Peterson-Nedry

ACKNOWLEDGEMENTS

This book is meant to showcase the personal stories of a handful of Oregon's many Willamette Valley winemakers. John and I owe a debt of gratitude to the participating winemakers for sharing the stories of their lives with us. They were so gracious. We cherish the work that came out of our time with these extraordinary people. We also cherish the experience on a personal level.

We would like to also extend our thanks to Matthew H. Hooper, JD, of the Seattle-based Foster Pepper PLLC law firm. As chair of Foster Pepper's Media, Entertainment and Games Group, Matt was an invaluable and highly responsive resource during the formative stage of this project.

Thanks to Dan Carr, who contributed to the marketing planning. Thank you to Tina Curry and Chris Cannard, the producers of wine festivals, including the Northwest Food and Wine Festival, for introducing me to The History Press. Thanks also to Baudouin DeMontgolfier, president of Tonnellerie du sud ouest, a French cooperage. This book's premise was inspired during a period when Baudouin and I were marketing his French barrels to Oregon winemakers. This work took me into the cellars, face to face with some of our many extraordinary winemakers.

Our local wine industry organizations responded to our deadline-drive requests for information despite their rigorous schedules. We are deeply grateful to Sue Horstmann, executive director of the Willamette Valley Wineries Association; Charles Humble, director of communications and interactive marketing, Oregon Winegrowers Association; and Rachael

Cristine Woody, archivist of the Linfield College Oregon Wine History Archive (OWHA).

We would also like to acknowledge those who helped coordinate interviews, select photography and provide editorial guidance and input.

A very special thanks to:

Kim Bellingar, Adelsheim Vineyard
Jane Box, Penner-Ash Wine Cellars
Matt Boyington, Willamette Valley Vineyards
Anna Campbell, Elk Cove Vineyards
John D'Anna, Cristom Vineyards
Laurel Dent, Ponzi Vineyards
Catherine Douglas, Adelsheim Vineyard
Jillian Glazer, Adelsheim Vineyard
Suzanne Oliver, De Ponte Cellars
Amy Robinson, Maysara Winery
Natalie Sigafoos, Lemelson Vineyards
Katie Wilson, REX HILL and A to Z Wineworks

Special thanks to John Vincent's talented wife, Lisa Holmes of Yulan Studio, for assistance with photography, page layout design and photo preparation.

A very special laurel for our History Press project editor, Ryan Finn, as well. Ryan shepherded "our baby" through the publishing equivalent of the "bottling process." He is a diligent wordsmith, accessible and collaborative. We very much appreciate having Ryan lead the book through these critical phases. We would also like to thank the photography department at HP, as well as our lovely History Press commissioning editor, Aubrie Koenig, and the editorial leadership at the company for taking a chance on us and on this book.

On a personal note for Vivian, a heartfelt thanks to my wonderful parents, Virginia Lynn and James George Schlesinger, for their encouragement at every step of the way. Thanks to George Asher Perry, Kristi Lopakka, Bonnie Biasi and Jim Ewald for the same. And thanks to my clan of altruistic "LPers" at Logical Position, a group of young Google people that collectively assured me that their generation is going to make this world a better place.

Thanks to Sarah Schlesinger for the illuminating illustrations in this book. She churned out everything in less than two months despite her extremely full schedule.

Above all, thanks to my writing partner, John Vincent. John came aboard this project at the onset of writing and was a relentless, equal contributor, always looking to take on more than his fair share, always rallying me toward the end goal and providing feedback and support at every stage. John is a hardworking professional and a cherished friend and colleague. It has been a tremendous honor to work beside him on this book.

—Vivian Perry

Chapter 1

HISTORY OF THE WILLAMETTE VALLEY WINE REGION

The history of Oregon's Willamette Valley Wine Region is a story of climate, soil, craft and culture. All these elements converge in a "perfect storm" for world-class Pinot noir.

Oregon is the third-largest wine producer in the United States behind California and Washington, and the Willamette Valley is the state's largest wine region, accounting for 74 percent of Oregon wine production and boasting more than three hundred wineries and 610 vineyards (some 16,800 planted acres), according to the Willamette Valley Wineries Association. The Willamette Valley's leading varietal is Pinot noir, but producers are captivating audiences with Pinot gris, Pinot blanc, Chardonnay, Riesling and Gewürztraminer, among some seventy-two other varietals.

The Willamette Valley American Viticultural Area (AVA) is a fertile triangular region more than one hundred miles long and up to sixty miles wide. Its shape is akin to a cluster of grapes, and its topography includes rolling foothills and valley expanses bordered by the Cascade and Coastal Mountain Ranges. The valley expands to the south and west from the state's largest urban center, Portland, pushing south through Salem to Corvallis and finally to Eugene. Its western edge is roughly fifty miles from the Pacific Ocean.

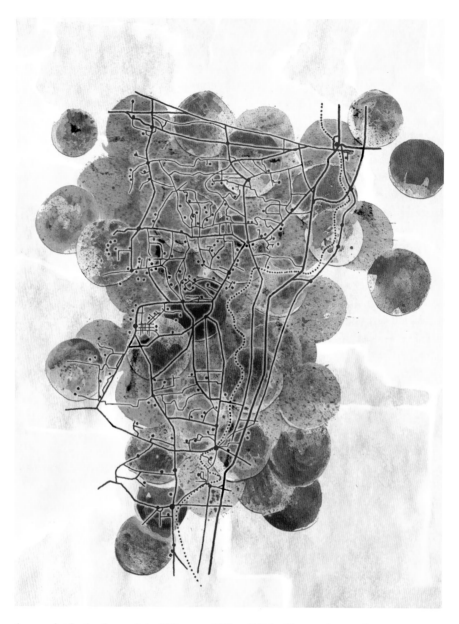

Appropriately, the shape of the Willamette Valley AVA is akin to a cluster of grapes.
Illustration by Sarah Schlesinger.

PERFECT CLIMATE FOR PINOT

The valley climate provides an elongated grape-growing season that is said to be ideal for Pinot noir. Winter is typically cool, wet and mild. Spring is oftentimes rainy, and summers are warm with cool evenings. An important distinction of the Willamette Valley is its location on the global 45th parallel—a geographic area considered to be an ideal climate for viniferous grape growing; it is said to provide the ideal balance of temperature, humidity and soil.

The 45th parallel is actually an imaginary line circling the planet. It is halfway between the North Pole and the equator. The thinking is as follows: if you go too far south or too close to sea level it is said to be too hot, and grapes can ripen so quickly that quality can suffer. If you plant too far north or at too high an elevation, it could be too cold for grapes to ripen successfully and predictably. France's Burgundy region, heralded for the most expensive and distinguished wines in the world, is also located within this imaginary band.

RICH GEOLOGICAL BREW

The Willamette Valley's rich soils are the beneficiaries of massive ice age floods called the Missoula Floods. Geologists estimate that some forty floods between fifteen thousand and thirteen thousand years ago left up to two hundred feet of rich, fertile sediment on the Willamette Valley floor and hillsides, according to John Eliot Allen and Marjorie Burns's *Cataclysms on the Columbia*, a noted book on the subject.

The floods swept topsoil from glacial Lake Missoula in Montana, through eastern Washington and down the Columbia River Gorge to the valley floor, according to Allen and Burns. These floodwaters drenched the entire Willamette Valley to heights of three hundred to four hundred feet above sea level before eventually draining off and leaving a valley floor rich in volcanic and glacial soil. The Willamette Valley Wineries Association identifies the region's main soils as marine sedimentary, volcanic basalt and windblown loess.

According to Allen, Burns and other geological authorities, Oregon State University geologist Ira S. Allison was the first to begin unraveling this story through his studies of similarities between the Willamette silt soil and a former lakebed in eastern Washington. Today, the former ice age lake is named in his honor as Lake Allison. Allison is also known for documenting hundreds of nonnative boulders, or erratics, that were carried to Oregon by these tremendous floods rafted on massive icebergs and deposited around the lower hills surrounding the Willamette Valley. One of the most prominent is the Bellevue Erratic, which is off Oregon Route 18, outside McMinnville, Oregon.

GRAPES ARRIVE WITH EUROPEANS

The first people of the Willamette Valley were indigenous Native Americans. The Calapooia tribes sustained themselves by hunting, fishing and gathering. Like so many other indigenous people, their exposure to New World germs was lethal. Historians note that in the early 1800s, 90 percent of their estimated population perished.

Lewis and Clark's 1807 expedition to Oregon spurred great interest in the fertile region known at the time as the Oregon Territory. Pioneers risked their lives traveling up to two thousand miles in oxen-drawn wagons along the treacherous Oregon Trail to reach this "promised land of flowing milk and honey," as it was publicized during those times.

It is thought that the early Oregon pioneers of European origin brought vines along. The first documented grapes were planted in Oregon's Rogue Valley in 1847. It was again in Oregon's Rogue Valley that the first commercial vineyard was planted in 1852 by Peter Britt. Another early wine pioneer was Ernst Reuter, who captured a medal for his Riesling at the 1904 St. Louis World Fair, all according to Rachael Woody, archivist at Linfield College, home to the Oregon Wine History Archive. The OWHA is an expansive public resource dedicated to documenting every facet of the Oregon wine industry and is administered through Linfield College's Nicholson Library in McMinnville, Oregon.

Woody explained that these earliest Oregon winemakers planted hundreds of acres of grapes and started producing profitable wines. Prohibition destroyed the emerging industry in its infancy. Anti-alcohol sentiment forced the closure and eventual loss of most of the wineries as Oregon was among the first states to adopt prohibition in 1913 and possibly one of the last to end it in 1933. Only a few survived by illegally bootlegging or making wine

Bordered by mountains and forests, the Willamette Valley sits on the 45th parallel and offers a perfect climate for growing grapes. *Chehalem.*

for religious ceremonies, according to archive documentation. Today, wine is emerging as a leader among the state's many agricultural products, which include greenhouse and nursery stock, wheat, hazelnuts, berries, vegetables, grass and vegetable seeds, Christmas trees and hops, which are widely used in the brewing of beer.

WINEMAKING AS ARTISAN CRAFT

Winemaking in the valley—in all of Oregon, in truth—is predominantly artisanal, or handcrafted with an eye toward creating world-class wines.

For example, most vineyards are located on hillsides because the industry producers know that this provides higher-quality grapes. To get tractors and other farm equipment up and down the slopes is more time consuming and costly, and the yields are considerably less, but the payback is quality and depth of character in the wines.

Hillsides provide more variations in soil types, rock subsurface and elevations that affect grapes and increase the winemaker's spectrum of flavor. Subtle climate differences at varying elevations also affect the grapes. In sum, it adds diversity and depth to the winemaker's spice rack. Hillsides also allow winemakers to extend their growing season because they offer better air circulation to cool the vines naturally. A long, slow growing season produces smaller grapes with higher-quality flavors. Vineyards planted on flat expanses are at risk of being baked by the sun and growing too quickly, according to the winemakers interviewed for this book.

Being good stewards of the environment is a mainstream lifestyle in Oregon and the Willamette Valley wine community. In truth, sustainable policies are all the rage throughout all of Oregon's wine regions. "It's a place where wineries are dedicated to sustainable winegrowing and winemaking practices based on their respect for the land and desire to see future generations continue the winemaking tradition," Woody said.

A whopping 47 percent of the state's vineyards are "certified sustainable acres," according to Charles Humble, director of communications for the Oregon Winegrowers Association. At that figure, Oregon leads the nation in this category. If you can make a correlation between earth-friendly practices and profit, and Humble does, the impact has been dramatic. "We do an economic impact study every five years. The last one was done in 2010 and showed that the impact was $2.7 billion annually. We loosely estimate that this number is now close to $3 billion."

STRUCTURING THE INDUSTRY

Handcrafted and sustainable practices at the vineyard level are buttressed by fervent public policy engagement to guide and secure the industry's collective goal to rise together and continue its journey in premier wine production. Since 2001, the Willamette Valley AVA has been divided into six new sub-AVAs, which are designated wine grape–growing regions within the United States. They are distinguishable by geographic features, with boundaries defined by federal authorities.

The six sub-AVAs in the Willamette Valley resulted from petitions, or formal requests, from within the wine industry. With more and more of these AVAs in place, smaller Willamette Valley regions are able to distinguish

Very high-quality Pinot noir is the signature varietal in Oregon's Willamette Valley, but other award-winners are grown here as well. *Adelsheim Vineyard.*

themselves to consumers. It is, in a way, a form of self-imposed certified marketing. If a label says the wine is from that AVA, it must be so by law. "Oregon got its ticket to the dance by taking its wine seriously," Humble said. To him, it is a significant chapter in the evolution of Oregon's wine industry. "It creates an identity for the kinds of wines and soils within an area."

The Oregon wine industry also rallied around the creation of a state labeling law to safeguard quality. The law states that a wine's origin and type must be properly labeled, according to Woody. The labeling law established a 90 percent minimum varietals content, meaning that in order to call it a Pinot, it has to be made from at least 90 percent Pinot grapes instead of the current national standard of 75 percent, she said. The same holds true for regional naming; if a wine is claimed to be from Oregon, at least 95 percent of its grapes must come from Oregon. Every licensed winery in Oregon had to sign off on the mandate in order for it to be approved by state regulators. "Such an effort quickly proved worthwhile as it raised the standard for Oregon wine and helped winemakers gain the trust and respect of the French, who recently had been frustrated by labeling misrepresentation in California," Woody noted. "Oregon benefited from this partnership when local winemakers had to rely upon the French for clone research and help with phylloxera epidemics."

Another grass-roots effort was the Table Wine Research Advisory Board, which was established to conduct research to support the young but growing wine industry. It received twelve dollars per ton, levied on grapes harvested in Oregon, and every winery in the state kicks in for the betterment of the industry on a statewide level. "They put upon themselves very stringent standards," Rachel said. "If it is called a Pinot noir, it has to be a Pinot noir. If they say it is from a certain AVA or region, those grapes have to be from that region. They knew they had to band together for the industry and they knew in doing so they would all be better off."

The sense of community is credited to the early founders of this industry, which arguably began in earnest in 1966. "Since the early pioneering days of the 1970s and 1980s, they were sharing everything from secrets to equipment. This unique combination of pioneering spirit and friendship has created a tight-knit community and top-quality wines. It amazes me every day I think of it," Woody said.

THE TURNING POINT

After prohibition, wine grape growing in Oregon was minimal. The turning point began with a 1952 thesis on cool climate viticulture written by Charles Coury. A favorite story from the early days is that of a Utah native who went to San Francisco in 1963 to study dentistry. He got sidetracked. In California's Napa Valley, David Lett became enthralled with winemaking. Two years later, after having read Coury's thesis, Lett and his wife, Dianna, were on their way to Oregon's Willamette Valley with what today looks like a treasure map. He came to Oregon for the growing conditions. He came to plant Pinot noir. Their first three thousand Pinot noir vines were planted on a southern slope in the valley's Dundee Hills. "I was convinced that these grapes belonged in this climate," said Lett in an interview with the Willamette Valley Wineries Association. The Letts produced their first wines in 1970. Coury was also establishing his vineyard here at the same time, although there is debate over which was first.

Only nine years later, in 1979, Lett would shock the international wine community. The World Wine Olympics, the Gault-Millau French Wine Olympiad, charitably allowed an entry from Lett's fledgling winery called the Eyrie. The Eyrie Vineyards captured an astonishing third place in this competition among the world's most prestigious and noted wines.

The French demanded a rematch a year later. A Robert Drouhin–sponsored French blind tasting reconfirmed the high ratings of the Eyrie Vineyards' 1975 Pinot noir. This time, Eyrie took second place—to a 1959 Chambolle-Musigne.

COMMUNITY AND QUALITY

Charles Coury and David Lett were among a handful of early wine growers, entrepreneurs with a passion for Pinot noir. In Oregon, we fondly call them "the founders." Some of them are featured in this book—Ponzi, Campbell, Adelsheim, Peterson-Nedry, Bernau and Sokol Blosser are names that evoke a sense of pride in Oregonians. They and many others have captured national and international attention for their great wines. "Somewhere along the way, they ultimately settled on how to be successful, and that was a relentless focus on quality," Humble said. "They were never going to build a Gallo, but they realized if they focused on learning, sharing [and] building community collectively, these small winemakers were going to make it."

The chapters that follow unfold the personal profiles of a wide range of the valley's winemakers in this industry that is still relatively young. At only forty-three years old, the wine industry is an important revenue generator in the state of Oregon. It is a remarkable collective win. As a transplant from the East Coast, it brings to my mind a recurring thought: "*only* in Oregon." This place is a national treasure.—VP

Chapter 2

ISABELLE DUTARTRE

WINNING A PERSONAL REVOLUTION

Isabelle Dutartre did not set out to become one of the finest winemakers in the world. She simply wanted to make wine. Because wine was so cool.

Isabelle is French. She grew up in a small village in Burgundy. She knew so many people who were into wine, and perhaps most importantly, her father loved the stuff. As a child, she would watch her father—and her grandfather—go down to the cellar to retrieve a bottle and then watch them return, holding their dirty prize, glass covered with dust, perhaps even disgusting looking. But the wine inside was so beautiful, so admired.

Isabelle did not wonder why this was so or recognize it as irony. She simply was captivated by it. And she wanted to be a part of it. It turns out that achieving her goal was a bit harder than it maybe should have been.

In the Beginning

It doesn't take much of a conversation with Isabelle to realize she has a spirit that always has longed to be free, regardless of her circumstances or any choices she has made. And although pragmatism marked her beginning in winemaking, it was her spirit that brought her career to life.

She began in a traditional way: in school, with studies in biology, followed by the winemaking program at the University of Dijon. But according to Isabelle,

Dundee Hills AVA is well known for its red clay/loam Jory soils. *Lisa D. Holmes.*

her true education didn't begin until she got a taste of the real world working at Maison Joseph Drouhin, one of Burgundy's highly regarded domains.

"It is not easy for a woman to become a winemaker in France, although it is getting better now, I think. But I was lucky. I met a woman at Drouhin, and basically she taught me everything I know. Because what you learn on the paper, it may be biology, chemistry, microbiology, biochemistry or whatever, but there is no soul in that. She gave to me this feeling like respect of the grapes and told me not to think you are going to change the world. You are simply going to make some wine. Yes, she taught me everything, especially tasting. I used to taste a lot. And then, you know, as you learn, it gives you the energy to do something with yourself."

Isabelle continued to work and learn at Drouhin in France for ten years. During that time, she met the man she would marry, but her husband (now her ex), an Australian and also a winemaker, was living and working in Bordeaux.

So, finally she left Drouhin, moved to Bordeaux to start a family and tried to find a job making wine.

BEGINNING AGAIN

"I moved to Bordeaux in January '92, and two months later, the owner of Drouhin called me and said, 'Did you find a job?' and I said no because you know if you are in Bordeaux and you are a Burgundy female

The view from De Ponte's winery, looking west across the Dundee Hills. *Lisa D. Holmes.*

winemaker, there is no chance you can find something. So he said, 'We need you for Oregon.' So I started to come here."

On the heels of Oregon's success in wine competitions, France's Maison Joseph Drouhin surprised the wine world by investing in a winemaking operation in Oregon's Dundee Hills. So, from 1993 to 1998, Isabelle flew to Oregon for harvests, racking and other critical winemaking events. It was a high price to pay when trying to raise a family, but her long-distance endeavors enabled her to stay connected with the wine business.

Between trips, she worked for a Burgundian cooperage firm in the south of France, where she moved in 1995, selling barrels, tasting the wine in barrels, trying to match barrels and different styles of wine. But after five years, it all became too much.

"In '98, I had enough. I had two kids, and it was a bit difficult. When they were really little, they came with me for harvest, but then with school and everything, it was too difficult, so I decided to stop traveling to Oregon."

As Isabelle recounts her story, it is easy to get a sense of the burden she carried—to feel her look inward and remember how hard it was, even though it's her nature to keep things light and use a bit of humor to convey her challenges. Unfortunately, things were not about to get easier. Even her next big opportunity carried a price.

After a year experimenting with making some merlot and cab in Bordeaux (clearly not a fulfilling time in her life), the owner of Oregon's De Ponte Cellars called and asked Isabelle to be its winemaker.

Isabelle's first reaction was to not go back. How could she? It had been too hard with two kids, and now she had three. But she missed her work making Pinot noir, and her husband encouraged her to go, to give it another try.

"So I took my baby, and I remember it was like three or four days after 9/11, one of the first planes to fly out after they reopened the airport. That trip was so much stress with all of the security, but anyway, I came with my daughter…she was like ten months old. Then I came back to Oregon and De Ponte for quite a while."

But once again, the strain became too much, and after another six years, which included a divorce and the need to juggle too many schedules, Isabelle knew that she had to make a decision.

After much soul searching, she chose to leave France and make Oregon her new home.

Putting Down Roots

Twelve years after she and her daughter experienced their first De Ponte wine harvest, Isabelle now feels at home in Oregon's Dundee Hills. Everything at De Ponte seems easy. The atmosphere is casual in spite of meticulously maintained vineyards and the apparent quality of the winery, including its recently renovated tasting room. It is the picture of understated elegance. It feels, in short, like the perfect place for Isabelle.

Looking lithe and somewhat ageless in her jeans and running shoes, she appears especially at ease in her lab, where she works to better understand her grapes and help them express themselves—much as a mother would help to guide her children.

A Mother's Love

Throughout her career as a winemaker, Isabelle has been defined by her attachment and commitment, both to her children and to her craft. In fact, it could be said that one endeavor actually helps to inform the other.

"I try to establish a relationship between my grapes and me. I talk to them and I touch them. I try to respect the grapes. Do not extract too much. Don't

DE PONTE CELLARS

De Ponte Cellars is located high in the Dundee Hills AVA of the Willamette Valley. Originally established in 1975, the vineyard is home to fourteen acres of Pinot noir and three acres of Melon de Bourgogne. The vineyards are planted to combine tried-and-true Burgundian formulas adapted to the unique Oregon terroir. De Ponte Cellars specializes in elegant and complex handcrafted Pinot noir produced with the utmost commitment to quality and sure to please a wide range of palates. The picturesque drive to the winery and tasting room winds through hillsides covered with manicured vineyards and puts you in the mood for some of Oregon's best Pinot noir.

YEAR FOUNDED: *1999*
OWNERS: *Scott and Rae Baldwin*
WINEMAKER: *Isabelle Dutartre*
VARIETALS: *Pinot noir, Melon de Bourgogne*

TASTING ROOM LOCATION:
17545 Archery Summit Road, Dayton, OR, 97114

HOURS: *open daily, 11:00 a.m.–5:00 p.m.*
FEE: *$10*
CONTACT: *(503) 864-3698*

SUSTAINABILITY FEATURES:
- *LIVE certified*
- *salmon safe*

ask for more than they can easily give. Be kind to them, and they will give you something back that is beautiful."

She continues, "It's like with kids. If you don't respect them, they won't respect you. I think with the wine it's the same. When something is wrong, you are here, but if everything is fine, then don't do anything. Just watch them and be sure everything is fine and keep them happy. If it is good, just let it go."

The winery and tasting room of De Ponte Cellars is nestled among its estate vineyards in Oregon's Dundee Hills AVA. *De Ponte Cellars.*

These are the words of a woman and an outlook that is clearly feminine. Does her experience influence how she—or any woman—would make wine? Isabelle believes that it does.

"I think about that a lot, and I think so, yes. I think women have more respect, and that is difficult to say because there are a lot of guys who have respect, too, but it's different for women. It's more like maternal love. For me, all of my wines are my babies. Sometimes during harvest, my daughter will call me and ask me to come to her volleyball game, and I say, 'You know I can't come; my babies need me. Remember when you were a baby? I was there for you, and now I must be there for these babies.'"

She adds, "But there are beautiful wines made by Oregon male winemakers, too. And I'm glad of that because it would be boring if we all made the same wine."

1789 WINES

1789 is Isabelle's own small boutique winery, with an annual production of about 150 cases—exclusively Pinot noir. It's the accomplishment of thirty years of experience in winemaking, in both Burgundy and Oregon. The grapes are selected from a high-quality vineyard and processed with respect and minimal handling. The result is a beautiful and classy Pinot noir, each one reflecting the personality of its vintage. 1789—"Oregon wine with a French accent."

YEAR FOUNDED: *2007*
OWNER: *Isabelle Dutartre*
WINEMAKER: *Isabelle Dutartre*
VARIETALS: *Pinot noir*

TASTING ROOM LOCATION: *none*

CONTACT: *(503) 435-7882; 1789wines@gmail.com*

LEADING A REVOLUTION

After spending years pursuing and ultimately achieving her dream of being an established and recognized winemaker, Isabelle took another step of creating her own label. And it's fitting that her personal wine, 1789 Wines, represents a revolution.

"You know, 1789 was the year of the French Revolution. I chose the name for that reason, for what it represents to me. And I love having my own wine. I can do anything I want with it—even give it away if I want to. But I also want to show people—I want to show my children—that you can do new things with your life at any time. I was older when I moved here, and it wasn't an easy thing to do. I want them to know that it doesn't matter what you're doing or how old you are. You can do something new with your life."

She concludes, "I wonder what is the next thing I will do. But for now, I am here. Making wine."—JV

Chapter 3

HARRY AND WYNNE PETERSON-NEDRY

A FATHER AND DAUGHTER STORY

S imply put, Harry Peterson-Nedry is a modern-day Renaissance man who got away with living life on his own terms. He is the founder and co-owner of Chehalem Wines. He is a former chemist, an active public servant to the wine industry, a writer, an acrylic artist and, perhaps most importantly, the father of a passionate, intelligent young winemaker who stops at nothing to further her knowledge of the art.

First planted in 1980, Harry's Chehalem Wines (pronounced chuh-hay-lum) is named for the surrounding Chehalem foothills. The phrase means "gentle land" or "valley of flowers" in the language of the area's first inhabitants, an indigenous American Indian tribe called the Calapooia.

Although Harry has been in the Pacific Northwest for forty years, his slight southern accent indicates that he is from elsewhere. The North Carolina native is the second oldest of four brothers. He was raised on North Carolina's Coastal Plain, and his family's history in the area dates back to the pre–Civil War era.

His spirit of adventure brought him to Oregon, and this strong natural bent was evident at age eight. At that time, Harry's first short story was published. It involved a young boy named Peter King who lived in the "Wild West" and whose parents had died, forcing him to face adult-like adversities and succeed against all odds.

Harry visited the West Coast as a teen (following "his" basketball team to the Final Four) and again during his college years on a National Science Foundation grant. After dual undergraduate degrees in chemistry and

English from the University of North Carolina, Harry worked for Union Carbide in Cleveland, Ohio. It was a prestigious position with unlimited potential for a chemist. With that said, Harry's spirit of adventure was stronger than the security of a global chemical company. After a few years, he saved enough money to rent a cabin in the remote wilderness of Index, Washington. He went there to write fiction and spent nine months doing so in his early twenties.

When asked why move so far away from his family and leave behind a promising career, Harry replied, "It was important to me to prove myself. I was the secondborn, with the firstborn's excellence thrown in my face all the time. I liked the idea of going far away and returning home with the mystery of the miles dripping from me. When you are away and doing things on your own and pushing the envelope, then you have stories to tell. It may be pedestrian among your peers, but when you go back home, you tell these stories that carry the magic of miles under your feet."

During his time in the remote cabin, Harry adopted a husky, fell in and out of love, ran out of money and faced a decision. "I was twenty-five years old and writing about life, but you don't know life until you have experienced life," Harry said.

Harry put his fiction to the side. He knew that he didn't want to be a T.S. Eliot, working all his life at a plain vanilla bureaucratic job just to write a great American novel. "Was I going to eventually succeed? Yes, because I was pretty good, but it was going to rip my guts out, and I was fairly idealistic. I was not in a state of mind to take rejections from publications, agents or editors. It would not have suited my twenty-five-year-old psyche."

Harry and his husky stayed in the Pacific Northwest, and he sought work in chemistry, which paid well for his top-shelf credentials. He obtained a chemistry position in which he applied his skills to the improvement of processes and the quality of products. The subject seemed to bore Harry so much I didn't stop him to ask where.

From 1973 to 1979, Harry was still hanging in there with what he described as a good and challenging position that did not entirely fulfill him. He married a woman who was writing about wine, and they both shared a deep interest and immersion in the subject that grew to a point that a new adventure emerged.

"From that point on, we hunted together for a piece of property," he said. They found it in 1980 and began planting in 1982. With a three-year-old son and a six-month-old baby girl, Harry and his wife, Judy, purchased 54 ridgeline acres that would later become part of the Ribbon

Ridgecrest Vineyard was the first estate vineyard developed by Harry Peterson-Nedry for his Chehalem winery. *Chehalem.*

A hillside vista from Chehalem's magnificent Corral Creek Vineyard. *Chehalem.*

Ridge AVA, thanks to a petition that Harry co-authored. They named this first of three estate vineyards Ridgecrest. Today, Chehalem consists of 263 acres of planted vineyards, including original vineyards and the Stoller Vineyards property owned by Harry's partner of twenty years, Bill Stoller.

Chehalem's first wines were introduced in 1990. Harry and Judy's two children grew up on the vineyard and took part in the work. At age eleven, their daughter, Wynne Peterson-Nedry, labeled Chehalem's first wines by hand, and it was a fond moment for her parents to reflect on. She took a lot of pride in that work. After high school, Wynne went to college and received an undergraduate chemistry degree, with a minor in poetry, from Bryn Mawr College in 2002. "I took the same path as him," Wynne said. "I went to school in Philadelphia and stayed out of Oregon for a while to experience other things."

Wynne spent a total of six years on the East Coast. After her undergraduate studies, she took a chemistry position in an upstate New York laboratory. During those years, Wynne would look forward to Harry's "care packages" that included such things as the vineyard harvest jacket, T-shirts and sneak previews of Chehalem wines. She came to know over that time that she wanted to return to Oregon. "I would visit, and there would be one of those sensory-memory connections from when I was growing up—like a rainy October night at 9:30 p.m. I was wondering why Dad was not inside watching *The Simpsons* with us, and I'd wander out to the winery, where he was working. He would show me what he was doing and teach me something, like how to punch down wine."

Wynne came back and obtained a research lab position at a local hospital system, Oregon Health and Science University (OHSU). She also began spending a lot of her free time helping out at Chehalem and soon came to a pivotal life decision: she would commit to a winemaking career. Wynne made Harry very proud the day she received her master's degree in viticulture and enology from UC–Davis in 2008. After harvest stints in New Zealand, Burgundy and California, Wynne returned home to Chehalem in 2009, where she accepted the post of assistant winemaker. In 2012, Wynne accepted the position of winemaker at Chehalem. While Harry is still involved, Wynne leads the winemaking efforts on a day-to-day basis. She also pursues opportunities to build on her knowledge. In the winemaking industry, in particular, it is widely understood that winemaking is a job in which you are continuously learning and adding to your toolbox. And a lot of that learning comes from peer-to-peer sharing.

CHEHALEM

"Chehalem" is an American Indian word meaning "gentle land" or "valley of flowers." The winery traces its history back to vineyard operations started by Harry Peterson-Nedry in 1980 at Ridgecrest Vineyards, the pioneering wine operation in Ribbon Ridge AVA, northwest of Newberg in Oregon's Willamette Valley. Equally well known for red and white wine quality, it carries a passion and focus for cool-climate varieties that reflect both site and climate in complex, structured and intensely fruited wines.

OWNERS: *Harry Peterson-Nedry and Bill Stoller*
WINEMAKERS: *Harry and Wynne Peterson-Nedry*
VARIETALS: *Pinot noir, Riesling, Chardonnay, Pinot gris, Grüner veltliner, Pinot blanc, Gamay noir*

TASTING ROOM LOCATION:
106 South Center Street, Newberg, OR, 97132

HOURS: *open daily, 11:00 a.m.–5:00 p.m.*
FEE: *$10–$15*
CONTACT: *(503) 538-4700; info@chehalemwines.com*

VINEYARDS:
- *Ridgecrest Vineyards (Ribbon Ridge AVA)*
- *Corral Creek Vineyards (Chehalem Mountains AVA)*
- *Stoller Vineyards (Dundee Hills AVA)*

To that point, Wynne was recently awarded a Rotary scholarship for a five-week educational exchange in Croatia. In May 2013, she and four other American industry professionals went there to share and gather knowledge from other winemakers. "They [Croatians] make a lot of white wines, and that interests me," she said, adding that Croatia's wine region is close to Austria, where they make a lot of Grüner Veltliner and Riesling wines. "While winemaking is relatively straightforward, you always learn something, and my Dad and I are very much Riesling fanatics and we love obscure things like the Grüner."

Chehalem's Ridgecrest Vineyard. *Chehalem*.

While this may sound like a geek's version of a glam lifestyle, Wynne was quick to temper anyone's temptation to think so. Winemaking involves continuous physical labor and continuous learning, she said, adding, "It is not a career you choose because you make a lot of money or you are famous," she said. "This mystery about some of us being rock stars is not true; it is a profession you choose because you love what you do. It is a profession of passion rather than wealth."

Today, Wynne leads the winemaking at Chehalem. Harry's time is partly spent on policy issues on the regional, state, national and international fronts. During our time together, Harry excused himself briefly to write an e-mail regarding a State of Oregon legislative measure dealing with wineries and their rights in rural areas. It was a bill that would affect the creation of boundaries that are fair and equitable to both rural farmers and their winery neighbors.

"The wine industry is growing strong, and we are all figuring out how to be good neighbors," he said. His e-mail was a communication to other wine industry founders active on the policy front to ensure that "we are all singing from the same sheet of music."

Harry has taken on leadership roles in numerous organizations and special initiatives to support the rapidly growing Oregon wine industry. His many years of "industry work" includes service on the Oregon Wine Board, the Willamette Valley Wineries Association, the International Pinot Noir Celebration, Oregon Chardonnay Alliance (ORCA) and Oregon Riesling Alliance (ORA), as well as international work with a focus on strengthening the geographic place name protections.

To Harry, the wine business in Oregon is a growing economic engine for the state that must be managed with thoughtfulness and purpose. "Candidly, the Oregon wine industry is a bridge between urban and rural interests," Harry said. "We are dealing with agriculture and nature, and we are also providing a luxury item that is world-class, something that excites the tattooed chef in Brooklyn."—VP

Chapter 4

LYNN PENNER-ASH

BREAKING BARRIERS AND EXPANDING BOUNDARIES

It's not easy being first. The pioneering winemakers who first ventured into Oregon's Willamette Valley found that out. These were men as well as husband and wife teams who broke new ground and paid the price—in sweat, hardship and risk—for their place in this state's winemaking history.

But as those pioneers began to expand their operations, and as new investors sought to grow the market and the dream, a new form of pioneer was needed: professionally trained winemakers, the people who could come in and take on the challenges of expansion and growth in an emerging market. Lynn Penner-Ash was one of the first of those second-wave winemakers. She also was the first woman among them. But please, don't focus too much on that fact.

"I don't want anyone to judge my winemaking from a gender standpoint. I don't want to be known as a great woman winemaker; I'm a winemaker, and that's it. Is it different for women? Let's just say it's been a little bit harder for women. They probably had to work harder to prove themselves, but that's slowly changing. I think maybe 15 percent of the winemakers in this area are now women. But I will admit it was a little weird coming up here from Napa, where I had a peer group of women involved in the industry, to [where] suddenly my peer group was the pioneers and a few other second-wave winemakers."

She adds, "At that time, the entire Oregon wine industry would sit in Nick's Back Room [Nick's Italian Café in McMinnville] and share a meal

The Penner-Ash winery and elegant tasting room offer an expansive and elegant spot to enjoy world-class wines. *Lisa D. Holmes.*

and talk about wine. And I was usually the only woman in the room. So where do you sit? It was definitely an adjustment."

LEARNING TO ADAPT

Learning how to fit in with her new peer group was only one of the challenges Lynn faced back in 1988 when she made her first Oregon wine. She also discovered that the industry here had no support structure—mostly because there really wasn't all that much industry to support. There are now well over four hundred wineries in Oregon, but when Lynn got here, there were fewer than fifty.

"Now you can call Davison's Wine Supply to get corks, yeast, whatever you might need, and he'll have it for you. But when I first got here, we'd have to go through the phone books and inevitably order what we needed from California, then wait three days for it to arrive before you could use that piece or component. So there were some very different early years. It was a very, very small industry with not a lot of support structure around it."

But it's not like Lynn to let something as small as a lack of business infrastructure stand in her way. To call her determined is probably something of an understatement. Besides, by the time she got to Oregon, she was used to dealing with obstacles.

After high school, Lynn went to UC–Davis to study botany. But after spending two years pulling apart flowers while wishing she was outdoors doing something else, she happily accepted a friend's invitation to spend a summer working on the crush deck at California's Domaine Chandon.

I'm sure everyone reading this profile knows what the outcome of that experience was: Lynn wanted to work in the wine industry. But here's the surprising part: she didn't want to make wine; she wanted to grow grapes.

"I loved working the crush deck that first summer. It was fun, it was exciting, it was full of young people who were all pretty much like-minded, and we just really, really enjoyed it. So I went back to Davis thinking that this combines botany and plant life cycles—things I love—but it's also outdoors. And the end product people enjoy so much more than what I was going to be doing in a botanical sense. So I went back to Davis and finished a degree in grape growing."

She adds, "Unfortunately, I ran into some gender hurdles in viticulture at the time. This was early '80s. Women were not well accepted into viticulture—the grape growing in the vineyards, the work in the fields. So I thought I could go in the back door by getting a winemakers degree. I initially saw it as a way to get to the vineyards, but once I got involved in the winery, it just was so exciting and so much fun and I really did love it. So ultimately, it turned out that the best decision for me was to stay in enology and winemaking."

A MOVE NORTH

Once she got her degree, she stayed in the Napa Valley and made wine there, initially scoring a job at Stag's Leap. Between her time at Stag's Leap and the time she worked between her viticulture and enology degrees, she had spent seven years learning to make wine in California.

Over that time, two things happened that helped shape Oregon's wine industry. The first was romantic. Lynn Penner met her soon-to-be husband, Ron Ash. The second was chauvinistic. Lynn was working at Stag's Leap as

Penner-Ash Wine Cellars is bounded by expansive views of the surrounding valley and vineyards that sweep down the hillsides. *Lisa D. Holmes.*

the enologist and had been allowed to make the off-site wines. But when it came time to hire a new assistant winemaker, she was not only passed over but also had to train the guy who was hired.

So, with Ron's encouragement, Lynn started looking around and putting the word out that she was interested in making a change. Somehow that word reached Paul Hart, the founder of Oregon's REX HILL Winery, who called her from Newberg and asked if she had any interest in interviewing for his position at REX HILL.

Lynn flew up and was hired within twenty-four hours. The combination of a completely supportive husband and a lack of career opportunity in California helped lead to the creation of some truly outstanding Oregon Pinot noir.

PENNER-ASH WINE CELLARS

Some buildings are more than just structures. The special ones give you a sense of place, a feel for the heart of the people who live and work in them, a tactile sense of the terrain on which they are built. The Penner-Ash winery, completed in 2005, is such a place. Nestled into a hillside overlooking the Chehalem Valley, the building seems to spring from the land itself and reflects the winery's values, spirit and winemaking philosophy. From inside the building, one has the illusion that the roof is floating, thanks to the wraparound clerestory windows revealing views of both Mount Hood and Mount Jefferson. Transparency also plays a large part in the layout of the winery design, built so the tasting room has a view of the winemaking space through the windows and to the outdoors.

YEAR FOUNDED: *1998*
OWNERS: *Ron and Lynn Penner-Ash*
WINEMAKER: *Lynn Penner-Ash*
VARIETALS: *Pinot noir, Syrah, Viognier*

TASTING ROOM LOCATION:
15771 Northeast Ribbon Ridge Road, Newberg, OR, 97132

HOURS: *open daily, 11:00 a.m.–5:00 p.m.*
TASTING FEE: *$15*
CONTACT: *(503) 554-5545*

SUSTAINABILITY FEATURES:
- *LIVE certified*
- *gravity flow design*
- *special ergonomic features*
- *energy conservation*
- *viticultural practices*

Creating a Label of Her Own

Lynn spent a number of years at Rex Hill, both making wine and helping to train a generation of Oregon winemakers. But in 1998, exactly ten years after joining Rex Hill, Lynn and Ron Penner-Ash produced 125 cases of their own Penner-Ash wine. And even though she continued on with Rex Hill until 2002, Lynn gradually—from 125 cases in 1998 to 14,000 cases in 2013—built her own Penner-Ash label into one of the most lauded wines in Oregon.

"I have to take a deep breath sometimes and look at it and wonder at what we've done, because we have been able to accomplish some pretty amazing things. But you know, you put your head down and you're trying to keep things going, keep ahead of the game, be involved, get your grape contracts lined up, get your bottling orders taken care of, and sometimes you get lost in the detail. So you do have to pull yourself out at times to take in the bigger picture. But it's starting to really hit home for us now."

She adds, "We both were in Chicago this past week, and there must have been 25 percent of a thousand-plus attendees who had been to our winery

A display of Penner-Ash bottles greets visitors to the winery's tasting room. *Lisa D. Holmes.*

or belong to our wine club. And you're just like…this is an amazing outreach that we have achieved. And for me, really, that just blew me away. We're in Chicago, and these people knew who we were. That was really fun."

She continues, "And people come into the tasting room and say, 'I love your wine,' or, 'I got married with a bottle of your wine,' and you realize that we're making twelve thousand cases times twelve bottles. That's how many people we're touching on a yearly basis now. So we take deep breaths and kind of go, 'Wow. It's pretty amazing.'"

All of Lynn and Ron's success happened a day at a time. They've joked with each other over the years that their motto should be "slow and steady" because they've never been the one-hit wonders who scored a fantastic write-up or review that put them in the limelight. Instead, they've slowly built a label that, year in and year out, reflects the skill, experience and artistry that comes from consistently being one of the best.

THE SECRET TO SUCCESS

Lynn says, "In winemaking, I like to think of our style as respecting what the vineyards are bringing us. And then making the choices, based on when and how the grapes come in, of what we need to do with them. Honestly, a lot of times, I know I frustrate whoever I'm working with because there are things I feel intuitively that we need to do, and I cannot honestly give you a reason for that. I may be out in the vineyard walking some morning, the sun is shining and something just comes to me. And I think, 'We need to do this and we need to do it now.' So I'll call in or come racing back and tell everyone what we need to do, and when my crew asks why, I simply say because it makes so much sense right now."

She concludes, "Is that thirty-plus years of experience or just intuition? I don't know, but it comes to me that this is what that vineyard is telling me to do, and so we do it and it seems to work."

But just in case you're wondering, this intuitive approach to winemaking has nothing to do with being a woman.—JV

Chapter 5

STEVE DOERNER

BRINGING OLD-WORLD STYLE TO OREGON WINE

It was 1978, and to put it simply, Steve Doerner needed a job. Here he was, a biochemistry major at UC–Davis who had come to realize that the 24/7 demands of medical school were not going to be a good fit with his easygoing approach to life. So what to do? Well, it's hard to be a student at Davis and not know about the viticulture and enology program, plus there were a lot of wineries in the area. It seems reasonable that Steve thought that winemaking might represent a possible path to a paycheck.

He went to one of his professors and asked if wineries ever hired biochemists. The answer was a pretty definite "no"; there were so many enologists graduating every year that even they couldn't all find spots. So Steve thought that maybe he'd just take a year off, travel to Europe and then go back to school until he could figure something out.

Two weeks later, his professor contacted him. A winery owner had just written to Davis seeking either a biochemist or microbiologist—he wanted someone who had *not* studied enology.

"So in 1978, mostly because I was in the right place and the right time, I got my start in winemaking at a place called Calera down in California." It turns out that the guy who hired Steve wanted someone who had a technical background but was unbiased about the winemaking process and would be open to taking more of an old-world approach.

"At the time, Davis was teaching—to their credit actually—sanitation, inoculation, filtration…things that elevated the quality of many wines. They advocated very safe, conservative, consistent winemaking, and because of that,

An aerial view of Cristom's Jessie Vineyard. *John D'Anna.*

they got rid of a lot of bad wine worldwide. But, if you followed that dogma or that recipe too closely, you would also be getting rid of some of the best wines in the world. They were trying to standardize the process and make it more of a science because that's what a university does. I don't want to bash Davis for that, but that's precisely what my employer was trying to avoid."

BUILDING ON TRADITION

Steve definitely wasn't biased. To be honest, he wasn't even all that interested. He just wasn't one of those people who was wild about wine, even though he grew up with it.

"My mother's side of the family is French, so we always had wine. Not great wine, by any means, but there was always a jug of wine sitting on the sideboard, and people would drink it until it was gone. Then it would get replaced. So I guess it was a part of our culture because it was included in meals, but it wasn't anything I ever thought about very hard."

CRISTOM VINEYARDS

Located in the rolling Eola Hills northwest of Salem, Oregon, Cristom Vineyards paints an idyllic picture as you drive through its vineyards to its winery and tasting room. Inside, you'll fine wines that have been recognized, nationally and internationally, as some of the very best in the Willamette Valley. Winemaker Steve Doerner and Vineyard Manager Mark Feltz have been on the property since day one, along with the founder, Paul Gerrie. Steve utilizes old-world, low-intervention winemaking techniques to produce wines that form a bridge between the Old and New World. He is a thirty-five-year practitioner of whole-cluster, native-yeast fermentations.

YEAR FOUNDED: *1992*
OWNERS: *Tom Gerrie, Steve Doerner, Mark Feltz, Christine Gerrie*
WINEMAKER: *Steve Doerner*
VARIETALS: *Pinot noir, Syrah, Pinot gris, Chardonnay, Viognier*

TASTING ROOM LOCATION:
6905 Northwest Spring Valley Road, Salem, OR, 97304

HOURS: *Tuesday through Sunday, 11:00 a.m.–5:00 p.m.*
FEE: *$5 per person, refundable with first purchase*
CONTACT: *(503) 375-3068; jeri@cristomwines.com*

SUSTAINABILITY FEATURES:
• *LIVE certified (winery and vineyard)*

And that was how Steve felt about wine. So it's safe to say that he had an open mind, which when combined with his technical capabilities allowed him to fully invest himself in his employer's vision. The outcome continues to inform the way Steve makes wine to this day.

"I basically learned that there's more than one way to make wine. My employer wanted to look to Europe or the Old World for insight. Obviously, because of my background, we did a lot of experimenting, but the goal was always to find out how little you could get away with. So even today, I bring that with me."

It was this same European influence that finally awakened Steve's passion for wine. He made his first trip to France in 1981 after having worked at the winery for nearly three years. It turned out to be a great journey. His employer's relationships enabled Steve to gain access to some of France's most renowned cellars, and in his words, he finally started to "get it."

"In the Burgundy region, you go to Beaune, and everyone's involved in the wine world in one way or another. It seems such a noble profession over there. It's all so beautiful, so historic. It's hard not to become completely enamored with it, quite honestly. If you want to start enjoying wine, just go someplace like that."

The trip also provided Steve with an introduction to one of his strongest winemaking influences. "The one guy who I probably try to model my winemaking after the most is a Burgundian named Jacques Seysses from Domaine Dujac. But I'm definitely not unique in that. He's probably influenced hundred of winemakers around the world just because he's so open-minded and willing to teach others, but his wines are delicious. And, by the way, he happens to use a lot of whole clusters."

Following his return home, Steve employed many of the techniques he learned in France. And when he joined Oregon's Christom Vineyards in 1992, the Willamette Valley benefited from his old-world influences and also gained a bit more whole cluster fermentation.

CREATING AN OREGON LANDMARK

Christom, located in the Eola-Amity Hills AVA a bit northwest of Salem, Oregon, presents a striking image to visitors with its attractive tasting room standing amid vineyards that sweep up the hillside. Its look of stability presents an accurate picture.

Purchased in 1992 by Paul and Eileen Gerrie, Christom still has its first winemaker in Steve Doerner and its first vineyard manager in Mark Feltz. "We've maintained a lot of stability here," says Steve. "It's one of the things that we're proud of…that and the fact that our wines are relatively consistent, although our style is a little bit unique. Our technique can make the wines a little bit hard when they're young—maybe a little more challenging to

The vineyards of Cristom Vineyards sweep across the Eola-Amity Hills AVA northwest of Salem, Oregon. *John D'Anna.*

A view of Cristom Vineyards as the sun rises over the Yamhill River. *John D'Anna.*

appreciate when they're first released. But it gives the wine longevity and ultimately more complexity, so that's why I do it."

Steve also feels like his techniques help Christom wines stand out in a crowd, and he appreciates the fact that Cristom has earned a reputation for making wines that age well. Over the course of his now thirty-six vintages, Steve has remained true to the simple, natural approach with which he began.

"Our winemaking is as hands-off as we can make it. That doesn't mean that I don't do anything because I try to make the best wine I can, and there are times when nature doesn't give you exactly what you need. I try to get the wines to be relatively balanced, so I make adjustments when I have to, but the goal is to not do it routinely. For example, we own a filter, but, knock on wood, we have never had to use it on our red wines."

Steve is clearly proud of the natural approach he takes to winemaking, but even so, he goes to some length to explain that he's not against employing technology. He simply opposes its automatic use. A good example of this is irrigation, a subject of much controversy in Oregon.

"We have relatively good rainfall here, but a lot depends on your soil type and what each growing season is like. We were completely dry-farmed through 2003, and that was a very hot, dry year, and I ended up having to put some water into the fermenters, which I hate to admit and don't like to talk about, but it made better wine."

He continues, "But really, if I'm going to add water, I'd rather put it on the grapes than in a fermenter, right? So after that experience, we identified three little areas on our property where we retroactively put some irrigation in. But it doesn't mean that we use it all the time. But now we have it, so if another '03 comes along, we'll be able to deal with it better. That's an example of technology that I don't advocate using unless you absolutely have to save your harvest."

Steve understands that not every winemaker shares his belief and that there are opposing schools of thought. Some winemakers use technology to manipulate every vintage into a signature style, while purists strive to assure that wine reflects its vintage, even to the point of making a wine that's out of balance. But he's comfortable finding the middle ground, doing what he must but striving to never overmanipulate. The key to this approach is the quality of the fruit. Good wine begins with good grapes.

"I've been really fortunate to work with great grapes. I believe wine's really made in the vineyard. A lot of people say that, but because we try to do as little as we can, I really do believe that. And I've been lucky to have the wines turn out pretty well without me having to work all that hard, which suits me pretty well, to be honest."

He notes, "Some winemakers just take themselves too seriously. They act like what they're doing is a really important job that requires special talent. But I find that it's actually not that difficult. People have been doing this for something like six thousand to ten thousand years, right? I mean, how hard can it be? It's just a process. It's natural. Grapes naturally want to turn into wine."

Steve concludes, "So sure, it's possible to make bad wine, and we all make mistakes. But really, if your one ingredient is grapes, and you manage to get the best grapes you can, then the winemaking part is relatively straightforward."

And I have no doubt that, after several decades of making outstanding wine, it should seem pretty straightforward.—JV

Chapter 6

DAVE PAIGE

THE CHALLENGER OF CONVENTIONAL WISDOM

In the early 1970s, a young couple named Ginny and David Adelsheim stood on a hilltop in the northern Willamette Valley to reflect on the dream they had just set in motion. They had purchased the land under their feet—fifteen acres of a sloped field rich with clay-loam soil and a gentle southern exposure. Today, David and Ginny's Adelsheim Vineyard is a point of pride for Oregonians. Among the first Oregon vineyards, Adelsheim has an international following.

The first thing to impart about Adelsheim is its mostly mispronounced name. And no one really cares at Adelsheim, but etymologically speaking, it is a combination of two German words that collectively mean "noble house," pronounced as "adels-heim" rather than what most folks call it, "adel-sheim."

"If you buy it, you can call it anything you like," said Adelsheim head winemaker Dave Paige. "It is better to be understood than correct." Dave is a fifty-year-old Cleveland, Ohio native. He made his way to Oregon as part of a deductive career path. The oldest son of five children, Dave's scientific nature is in step with family tradition. His father was a General Motors engineer who taught himself how to use the ancient nautical navigation tool, the sextant, as part of a new hobby in boating.

Dave's undergraduate studies at Ohio State began with a misstart, and he left without graduating from biochemistry studies to work in a wine shop. "When I was studying in science class, I missed having the creative outlet, and when immersed in something more creative, I sort of felt there was this other set of attributes that were not tapped into," he said.

Adelsheim winemaker Dave Paige joins harvest workers at the conveyor to sort grapes. *Adelsheim Vineyard.*

Adelsheim Vineyard winery and tasting room. *Lisa D. Holmes.*

At the wine shop, Dave developed a knowledge of and appreciation for the complexities of winemaking and how they required a confluence of creative, mathematical and scientific intellect. "At the time, I would have said this is a big enough topic not to get bored," said Dave. "If I had any common sense, I would have studied computer science, headed out to Silicon Valley, and I would be owning a couple wineries today."

Dave Paige reentered undergraduate studies at University of California–Davis for a Bachelor of Science degree from the viticulture and enology program. He knew within months that it was the right thing to do. It was engaging both sides of his brain simultaneously and therefore not boring him or forcing him to turn off one mental aspect for another.

After graduation, Dave landed a job at the mega-vineyard Sterling Vineyards in California's Napa Valley, where he worked in the laboratory for three years. It was a very big winery, a place where there was lots of lab work, and it was an interesting experience and opportunity to think about the role of data in winemaking. "I was doing nothing but generating data," he said. "How are we using this data? How much of it is used in decision-making? Things like that are opportunities to learn why you are doing what you are doing. I'd always ask what part of this matters?"

Reflecting on that period, Dave said that a lot of that data was a waste. He saw firsthand what went up the "food chain" and became an impactful part of the decision-making process. In truth, a lot of the information he was generating was not well reasoned but served an emotional need of making people feel good "because I have all this data."

Dave's next career step included a harvest stint in Australia followed by an assistant winemaking position at a small California winery, where he would take on a role that required him—for the first time in his career at age thirty—to be the wizard behind the curtain, to take an active part in the experiment of making wine and all its complexities. This experience was with Jeckel Vineyards in Greenfield, California, in the Salinas Valley.

During Paige's tenure at Jeckel, growth was substantial; when he walked in the door, they were selling forty-five thousand cases per year, and that number had tripled by the time he left.

Dave and his family came to Oregon when Dave was offered the head winemaker position at Adelsheim. While in Monterey, California, Dave met and married his wife. She is a Monterey native and the former director of catering for the Monterey Bay Aquarium. As such, the Paige family returns

ADELSHEIM VINEYARD

For more than forty years, Adelsheim Vineyard has been carefully cultivating vineyards and making wines sustainably in the Willamette Valley. It is a leader of the Oregon wine industry, dedicated to consistently producing and selling wines crafted in a style that centers on elegance, complexity and richness in flavor and texture. Established in 1971 by David and Ginny Adelsheim, the Adelsheim Vineyard estate has grown to include eleven exceptional vineyard sites in the north Willamette Valley, totaling 229 acres. Today, David leads a new generation of passionate staff devoted to leading the industry in crafting consistently alluring wines.

YEAR FOUNDED: *1971*
OWNERS: *David Adelsheim, Ginny Adelsheim, Jack and Lynn Loacker*
WINEMAKER: *Dave Paige*
VARIETALS: *Pinot noir, Pinot gris, Pinot blanc, Chardonnay, Auxerrois, Syrah*

TASTING ROOM LOCATION:
16800 Northeast Calkins Lane, Newberg, OR, 97132

HOURS: *open daily, 11:00 a.m.–4:00 p.m.*
FEE: *$15*
CONTACT: *(503) 538-3652; info@adelsheim.com*

VINEYARDS:
- *Anna Louise (Eola-Amity Hills AVA)*
- *Boulder Bluff (Chehalem Mountains AVA)*
- *Bryan Creek (Chehalem Mountains AVA)*
- *Calkins Lane (Chehalem Mountains AVA)*
- *Fennwood (Yamhill Carlton AVA)*
- *Hillside (Chehalem Mountains AVA)*
- *Quarter Mile Lane (Chehalem Mountains AVA)*
- *Redman (Ribbon Ridge AVA)*
- *Ribbon Springs (Ribbon Ridge AVA)*
- *Richards (Chehalem Mountains AVA)*
- *Stephens (Eola-Amity Hills AVA)*

to the area to visit family. "When we go back to visit, we still see it as beautiful, but we know we are going back to somewhere beautiful."

When they sat down together for an interview, Dave Paige and David Adelsheim discovered that they shared a foundational, albeit controversial, vision of wine strategy that challenged the conventional wine critics' ideals of great wines. "It was very clear to me in our conversations that we both had the feeling that the Pinot noir we wanted would be complex and elegant rather than 'mouth filling, densely structured wine.' We like it bigger, too, but not at the expense of complexity and elegance."

At Adelsheim, the Daves' trust in their shared path has paid off in awards and recognition. It took time, but over the years, Adelsheim has enjoyed positive reviews and high scores from the wine press. In a way, it seems as if the wine critics have become more accepting of the new paradigm that focuses more on the wine consumer than the critic and acknowledges that people typically open a bottle of wine with food.

"It excites me to some extent that the wine press is more and more appreciative of what we are trying to do: a finesse-driven and elegance-driven, fascinating wine. That is just as important as a great, opulently dense mouth wine," Dave said. In a sense, Dave feels that Adelsheim has been a change agent. "There are others like us sticking to our guns."

Dave's strategy is to continually seek new ways to improve by creating experiments in the vineyard that one can track. There is so much general knowledge gained in experimentation, and Dave's microbiology background is a safeguard against the "snake oil salesmen who try to dazzle you with bad ideas." Alas, it is not foolproof. "Science bring us someplace and drops us off to figure it out," he said.

Another Oregon anchor is the community. Here in Oregon, there is collaboration among winemakers that would make most people wonder why. "There is this sense that we are all in this together," said Dave.

For example, in the early days, winemakers/winery founders would assist one another during harvest and lend one another equipment. Paige was shocked to see all the archival pictures of them all working together in one another's vineyards. There are also long-established conferences today, such as the Steamboat Wine Festival, where winemakers meet to share ideas on how to make Pinot noir. "It is always a brutally honest discussion; we all bring a barrel sample and spend an entire morning in blind tastings. It is sixty winemakers in a room, and typically, we usually bring a sample of a screwed-up wine. We all taste it and provide insight

Willamette Valley winemaking pioneer David Adelsheim (right) with his winemaker, Dave Paige. *Adelsheim Vineyard.*

on how to fix it. At night, we drink each other's wines and continue to talk about it all," Dave said.

Oregon has its challenges, too, and perhaps that is why the winemakers rally to assist one another. For example, the confluence of environmental factors and topography almost makes it predetermined that the region should produce a higher-price, quality wine. The vineyards in the Willamette Valley are mostly planted on the slopes, which produce better grapes at half the yield of a flat square mile of vineyard. The slopes allow for better ventilation and better soils. The growing season is long and cool and wet. Getting equipment to these swaths of sloped vineyards and maintaining them is more time consuming and expensive than it is on the flat valley floors of neighbors such as Walla Walla and California, which produce up to double the grape yields at least.

Likewise, sustainable practices are the norm in Oregon. If you know anything about Oregonians, you will believe Paige when he says that Oregon's challenge was in getting state wineries to promote those practices. "We have to beat them in doing something special," Dave said. "Most of us believe that, and it becomes part of the glue that keeps us together—

even our Willamette Valley Pinot noir retails for thirty dollars, so the bar is pretty high."

Should he retire at sixty-five, Dave reasoned, he would have had thirty-five vintages in his lifetime. He obviously cherishes every one. "If I waste five of those on dumb ideas, it is a crime. This isn't brewing; I don't get grapes again until next year."—VP

Chapter 7

LUISA PONZI

LAYING THE GROUNDWORK FOR FUTURE GENERATIONS

Perspective is everything. For many wine lovers out there, the idea of growing up in Oregon's Ponzi winemaking family sounds fascinating, maybe even amazing. But for a young girl who, like most kids, wanted more than anything to simply fit in and feel normal, it was just plain embarrassing.

Luisa Ponzi was three years old when her parents, Dick and Nancy Ponzi, decided to leave California's Bay Area behind and start a new life in rural Oregon. It's a romantic story, really. Two Californians—hippies at heart—who chose to leave a successful engineering career behind and find a place where they could raise their three young children on the land—raising animals, growing a vineyard, making wine and giving their kids a simple, wholesome life.

So, the Ponzis settled on eleven acres in the Willamette Valley southwest of Portland. They planted their first vineyard in 1970, a time when almost no one in the area was growing grapes or making wine. Again, perspective counts.

"When I was growing up, I really didn't want to tell my school friends what my parents did because it was so strange. I mean, my family was making alcohol. But it wasn't just the stigma of that; it's that we didn't want to be different, and we were so different. Other kids just couldn't quite get their heads around it. I remember when we'd plant a new vineyard, we'd put milk cartons around the plants to protect them. And that was the comment when I got on the school bus...'What are you guys growing...milk?' And it was just like, 'Oh God, I can't even explain this.'"

Luisa (right) and Maria Ponzi represent the second generation of one of Oregon's pioneer wine families. *CWK Photography*.

The fact is that Luisa's concerns went far beyond any social stigma. It was the work. It seemed like her life was always a lot of work. Weekends were spent in the vineyards or the cellar, and there was rarely any downtime.

"We not only didn't ever go to Mexico or Hawaii, we didn't go anywhere. We had to work. If we got a week off of school, we worked. And growing up, those were my thoughts about winemaking: incredibly hard manual labor, washing the floors, cleaning the drains, usually very cold and dirty."

At the time, Luisa didn't realize how much working in the vineyard with her family was shaping her perspective, her sense of season and her love of nature. She did love the time her family spent together, and truth be told, she had a lot of fun, but she didn't understand that her parents, without really setting out to do so, were helping to create an industry. And that meant dedication and work. But nothing changed her impression, as a child, that she was living through the struggle of pushing something uphill for a long, long time.

"By the time we finished high school, for all of us—me, my sister and my brother—I think we all were really keen to get as far away from working in a vineyard as we possibly could." Luisa's brother left for Los Angeles to pursue a career as a musician, her sister ended up on the East Coast working in marketing and Luisa, being a lifelong science kid, left for college to study biology and prepare for medical school. But as it turned out, college wasn't exactly a smooth process either.

She spent a few years at the University of Oregon, went down to Pomona College for a year and then settled in at Portland State and ended up studying both biology and English literature. But even though she had wandered a bit and developed some doubts, Luisa still had her sights set on medicine, so she went to work at OHSU in the dialysis unit while she sent in applications to med schools.

"Honestly, I accepted the opportunity at OHSU because I felt like I needed to check the atmosphere in a medical environment. At that point, I was starting to wonder if it was going to suit me. And in fact, what very quickly became clear was that I wasn't cut out for medicine. It was just so rigid and sterile and just didn't feel right. So at that point, I was at a loss and didn't know what I was going to do."

It was the end of summer in 1991 when Luisa left her medical dreams behind and accepted her father's invitation to come home and work the harvest. This would give her something to do while she figured out her next career move. But what came next turned out to be a huge surprise.

"He was very clever, my dad. He put me in charge of the lab for that vintage. And that was the first time, after twenty-some years, that I realized there was science to winemaking. I just never got that before, that it wasn't just hard work. There was actually this whole scientific, creative part that went along with it. It was really cool to know I could create something based on science."

Luisa was smitten. Everything finally made sense, and she knew she was on the right path. But she also knew that if she was going to follow in her father's footsteps, she should go get some education. Especially as a woman, she believed that she needed to bring some credentials to the table and not just learn from her dad.

She considered going to UC–Davis to get a degree in fermentation sciences, but she felt that Davis focused too much on California wines and wasn't as applicable to what was happening in Oregon. Burgundy felt like the better place to study. So she spent the next eighteen months studying viticulture and enology in Beaune, France, and working in wineries in France and Italy.

Then, in 1993, she came home and took over the winemaking job at Ponzi. It was a long journey back to the wine farm, and it turned out to be the same journey both of her siblings had made, as well.

Harvesting Ponzi Pinot noir grapes. *Polara Studio.*

"We all came back. I guess the pull was just too great. I suppose it's a pretty classic tale of the next generation of a new business or industry in that it really is hard to escape. It becomes so much of what you are that you're tied to it on a certain level. When I talk to my peers who are also next generation, it's very similar, but in my mind, it was a surprise. This wasn't at all what I planned."

Now, twenty vintages later, Luisa is quick to confirm that coming home was the right choice. She loves everything about her life at Ponzi Wines. But then, life at Ponzi has changed over the past couple of decades. "We were still quite small when I started. We were doing maybe a thousand cases a year, and now we're at about fifty thousand cases, so we've grown quite a lot."

What challenges does change like that create for a winemaker? It means that if you hope to maintain any kind of consistency, you learn to adapt. "My father was making great wine when he brought me into the lab and got me started, so when I took over the reins, it wasn't like I was going to come in and fix something. Sometimes I get asked, 'How did you make your mark?' and I don't know that I have made my mark. The main thing I've done is maintain the great wines that he was making and just expand what we were doing."

PONZI VINEYARDS

Thriving under the second generation for more than two decades, this family-owned and family-operated winery is internationally acclaimed for crafting some of the world's finest cool-climate wines. For more than forty years, Ponzi Vineyards has set the standard for New World Pinot noir production with innovation in gravity flow and gentle handling techniques. All 120 acres of Ponzi vineyards and the state-of-the-art, thirty-thousand-square-foot winemaking facility are certified sustainable, recognizing the winery's commitment to environmental responsibility. Ponzi Vineyards continues to set the bar for Oregon wines and remains at the forefront of the nation's top wine producers.

YEAR FOUNDED: *1970*
OWNERS: *the Ponzi family*
WINEMAKER: *Luisa Ponzi*
VARIETALS: *Pinot noir, Chardonnay, Pinot gris, Pinot blanc, Riesling, Arneis, Dolcetto*

TASTING ROOM LOCATIONS AND HOURS:
Ponzi Vineyards—19500 Southwest Mountain Home Road, Sherwood, OR, 97140; open daily, 11:00 a.m.–5:30 p.m.
Ponzi Historic Estate—14665 Southwest Winery Lane, Beaverton, OR, 97007; open Wednesday–Sunday, 10:00 a.m.–5:00 p.m.
Ponzi Wine Bar—100 Southwest Seventh Street, Dundee, OR, 97115; open daily, 11:00 a.m.–5:00 p.m.

FEE: *$15–$20 per person*
CONTACT: *(503) 628-1227; info@ponziwines.com*

SUSTAINABILITY FEATURES:
- *LIVE certified (winery and vineyards)*
- *salmon safe*
- *carbon reduction challenge*
- *gravity flow winemaking process*
- *extensive sustainable features in facility and operations*

Ponzi's elegant new tasting room and state-of-the-art winery. *Adam Bacher Photography.*

The Ponzi expansion under Luisa's guidance has included planting more vineyards and buying a lot of fruit. It also includes the construction of the family's new winery and tasting room, as the business has migrated over the years from its original garage-sized winemaking endeavor to become one of the larger operations in the region. With that kind of expansion, Luisa's methods had to change, which makes it that much more admirable that she has been able to sustain the intrinsic character of Ponzi wine.

"Initially, this was much more of an academic endeavor for me. It was much more about the science and the analysis of it all, but now it's intuitive. It's so much more intuitive that I really don't even look at numbers that much anymore. In fact, it's become less and less about the science and more about the art. Which is wonderful, I think. Maybe it's this way in everything… when you become better at what you're doing, you don't have to think about it as much. It's nice to have that confidence."

She adds, "The difference in the wine I don't think has changed dramatically. The character of the wine, the style of the wine, I feel, is very consistent. And we've remained true to our goal, which is to do as little as possible to the wine, to maintain a consistency to our wines through blending rather than manipulation. I feel like I'm really here to keep things on track. To make sure that we are producing wine that is consistent to what my father did before me and that it's something people out in the world can identify. They see the name 'Ponzi' on the label, and they understand what that wine's about. I'm kind of holding the spot for whatever comes next."

Luisa feels that her job as a next-generation winemaker is not to completely change everything. More so, it's to make sure that things don't go downhill.

Make sure the quality is still high. Innovate when possible, and keep things fun and challenging. Her overarching goal is to make certain that what the winery is doing now will bode well for the generations to come.

"That means that our farming practices need to be as organic as possible. How we make wine must be a sustainable, economical endeavor. I'm very mindful that this isn't about me. It's about this business and keeping it going for generations. So it's not an ego thing, whereas sometimes I think wineries can become kind of ego-driven. For us, we're pretty mindful that this is a lifestyle. It's something that we love to do, and we need to maintain it for the next generation and all the generations to come."—JV

Chapter 8

ADAM CAMPBELL

PICKING UP WHERE THE PIONEERS LEFT OFF

Adam Campbell is a forty-two-year-old winemaker who has arguably been in the wine industry for thirty-nine years. At age three, Adam arrived at an abandoned prune farm in Gaston, Oregon, along with his parents and four siblings. There was no grand tasting room and no orderly planted fields of grapes. Nor was there a house for warmth, just 112 acres of picturesque foothills buffered by a vast wilderness of thousands of acres, an area still inhabited by magnificent wildlife today, such as bear, mountain lion and elk.

When his parents happily exclaimed that they were at their new home, Adam's question was "Where is it?"

"It is right behind us," they answered.

The Campbell family arrived at their newly purchased homestead with a trailer in tow. Adam, his siblings and parents (Elk Cove founders Pat and Joe Campbell, thirty-two and thirty-five years old at that time) all lived in the trailer during their first winter, which was "cold and a little miserable," according to Adam.

In the summers, Adam's two stepbrothers would join the fun. They would all sleep outside under the stars on the hilltop where a magnificent winery now sits. During those early days, the family woke up one morning to find a herd of Roosevelt elk bedded down in the cove just below their hilltop campsite, not more than one hundred yards from them, and the vineyard was easily named "Elk Cove."

Elk Cove Vineyards rests within a scenic natural landscape bordered by the Oregon Coast Range. *Lisa D. Holmes.*

The son of an emergency room doctor who married his high school prom date, Adam has taken his family winery from an original 50 planted acres to 250 since his leadership began in 1999. He explained that his parents took a courageous "leap of faith" during their tenure and that it only makes sense to continue that tradition. With reverence for his parents' thoughtful decisions, he said, "My parents have been the best partners in that. There were times when we were buying new properties, and I had to have a pretty good plan and they had to have a lot of confidence in me. If I am going to be as successful as they were, I need to be entrepreneurial and motivated and expand on what they did."

Adam's mom, Pat, grew up on her parents' pear farm in Oregon's Hood River Valley. She is a first-generation American of Swiss decent, like most of the folk who settled in the community. In fact, the universal German dialect "Swiss-German" or "Swiss-Deutsch" was taught in her elementary school. Pat grew up among a tight-knit family of farming aunts and uncles. Many of them are still farming in this fertile valley in the shadow of Mount Hood.

Joe was raised in the Hood River Valley, too, but his parents owned and operated a motel, which is where he grew up. His family was of modest means, but Joe was smart and hardworking. He received a full scholarship

ELK COVE VINEYARDS

Founded in 1974 by Pat and Joe Campbell, Elk Cove Vineyards is one of Oregon's oldest and most respected wine producers. Estate vineyards now cover more than 250 acres on five separate sites in the northern Willamette Valley. Steep, south-facing slopes with well-drained soils provide the perfect environment to grow the world-class wine grapes that are handcrafted into Elk Cove's wines. In 1995, Adam Campbell joined forces with his parents to make Elk Cove a multigenerational, family-run operation. As winemaker and general manager, his contribution to Elk Cove Vineyards is based on a love for handcrafted wines and a commitment to excellence.

YEAR FOUNDED: *1974*
OWNERS: *Pat and Joe Campbell, Adam and Carrie Godlee-Campbell*
WINEMAKER: *Adam Campbell*
VARIETALS: *Pinot noir, Pinot gris, Pinot blanc, Riesling*

TASTING ROOM LOCATION:
27751 Northwest Olson Road, Gaston, OR, 97119

HOURS: *open daily, 10:00 a.m.–5:00 p.m.*
FEE: *$5*
CONTACT: *(503) 985-7760; info@elkcove.com*

VINEYARDS:
- *Elk Cove Estate Vineyard (Yamhill Carlton AVA)*
- *Mount Richmond Vineyard (Yamhill Carlton AVA)*
- *Five Mountain Vineyard (Chehalem Mountains AVA)*
- *Clay Court Vineyard (Chehalem Mountains AVA)*
- *Windhill Vineyard (Willamette Valley AVA)*

to Harvard University for undergraduate medical studies. Adam explained that Joe also had "great teachers" who saw his potential and groomed and encouraged him. Joe would later graduate medical school from Stanford University in California to become an emergency room doctor, a position that would later become a means to an end in pursuit of his dream of building a winery with Pat, once the fifteen-year-old girl he took to his high school prom.

Pat and Joe went separate ways after high school. Both of their first marriages fell apart, and they crossed paths in the California Bay Area in their late twenties. The rest is history. They married and had three children, but there was a total of five children in the summertime, as Joe's two sons from his previous marriage would join the fun at Elk Cove.

The early years of their marriage took place during the Vietnam War era, and Joe was an objector. He was drafted as a doctor, and while he was not going to run to Canada, he was not going to participate in a war he thought was senseless. Luckily, the military offered him an alternative assignment to spend two years as a medical doctor on an Indian reservation in South Dakota. Adam was born on the Sioux Nation's Pine Ridge Indian Reservation, a place once inhabited by the notable Native American Indian warrior Crazy Horse, the fearless Indian leader who took up arms against U.S. troops in the 1870s and won in the Battle of the Little Big Horn. The battleground is on the site of the Pine Ridge Reservation. After Joe served his full two years, the family moved back home to Oregon.

Pat's father, Grandpa Menz, made a good living as a pear farmer, but he watched the competition from imports grow over time, commoditize the industry and cause profit margins for local farmers to deteriorate. When his daughter and her husband approached him with the idea to start a winery, he stood behind Pat and Joe. "Grandpa was supportive of doing something different, bringing in their love of wine and having a value-added product that you can have more control over than pears, which we would sell to packing houses," Adam said.

The Campbell family worked very hard in those early days. Joe was lucky enough to get an emergency room position of two, double-back-to-back twenty-four-hour shifts, which allowed him ten days off for planting vines, growing grapes and making Elk Cove's first wines alongside Pat. After ten years of this schedule, Joe was able to give up the emergency room work and focus on the winery, with occasional volunteer medical missions to poverty-stricken areas of the world such as the Sudan and Sri Lanka. In 1999, Pat and Joe retired and put Adam in charge of Elk Cove Vineyards. Today, Joe enjoys doctoring the underprivileged as a part-time volunteer, and both Pat and Joe still help out at the winery.

Adam and his four siblings grew up exploring the vineyard and the wilderness surrounding it. They had horses, cows and chickens and also

Elk Cove Vineyards' winery and tasting room offer an oasis amid the foothills and forests. *Lisa D. Holmes.*

worked in the vineyard. "We were all our parents' first labor force. It was fun, but we worked every day," he said, adding, "It's not like they [Pat and Joe] were out there watching us drinking ice tea; they worked very hard as well."

When it was time for school, Adam enrolled in Oregon's Lewis and Clark College and majored in political science to receive a Bachelor of Science degree. He traveled throughout Europe when afforded the opportunity, and among the places he visited was a family-owned winery in Alsace, France. During that time, he bonded with a young man his age who was certain he would one day lead his own family's vineyard. "That got me thinking," Adam said. "I loved Alsace, walking through the vineyard and seeing his excitement in taking over for his family's winery."

Other pieces of Adam's life came together during his college years. Backpacking through Europe with American friends, they met a group of like-minded Australians on Rome's Spanish Steps. The two groups took an immediate liking to each other and decided to continue their journey all together. Among the Australians was a girl named Caroline. She would later become Adam's pen pal, then his wife and then the mother of their

Elk Cove Vineyards' tasting room offers balcony views of manicured vineyards and rugged forests. *Lisa D. Holmes*.

three children. Adam put a shoulder to the mission when he went to Sydney, Australia, for studies. "I convinced her to come back here with me eventually."

As the winemaker and owner of Elk Cove Vineyard, Adam's time is divided between duties such as winemaking, overseeing all operations, land acquisition and traveling to promote Elk Cove wines. When time permits, he enjoys socializing with friends and family. For example, the night before our interview, Adam's wife and children all went to Luisa Ponzi and Eric Hamacher's home for a dinner party. Luisa made fresh pasta. Dave Paige, of Adelsheim, was also there with his wife. All three winemakers brought a bottle of their 2012 Rose, while the kids played together and their spouses joined in the fun.

The experience of the Willamette Valley in general is a very personal one. Any visitor will find that it lacks the corporate-owned feel. You can actually visit a winery and find yourself in the cellar with the winemaker or in the garden talking to a founder. Adam said with a laugh that once he met a visitor who walked into the tasting room and told him that she had just met his gardener and that she was a really lovely lady. "I just smiled, but I felt like saying that lovely lady is the founder of this winery." It was Pat, of course.

When asked what he thinks about most, Adam said his children. "My wife and I will bring them to the winery on Sundays, and we all work together. They are young, and they think about professions such as firefighters and teachers, and I am slowly trying to let them see the potential for being part of the wine community. I'm secretly hoping one of them will take over where I leave off."—VP

Chapter 9

ERIC HAMACHER

WORKING TO CREATE NEW OPPORTUNITIES

Vision is often born of a deep desire to realize a lifelong dream. Other times, vision grows slowly within a fertile, patient mind and is shaped by a person's ability to observe and understand a situation and then synthesize a new idea. Eric Hamacher's vision fits both these descriptions. And Oregon's wine industry has benefited because of that.

Eric first came to Oregon to make "mind-blowing Pinot," but when he got here, he discovered that the state's still young wine industry wasn't set up to accommodate young winemakers with big dreams but limited means. So, he set about finding a solution, fueled by a passion that had been simmering for years.

LOVE AT FIRST TASTE

Eric first met Pinot noir during high school. The impression it made was indelible. He was working in high-end California restaurants, mostly around Carmel and Monterrey. He liked the work, especially at the end of the night, when everyone was tipping out the busboys, and the guys who had spent the evening selling Cabernet would buy a good bottle of Burgundy for the staff meal.

The Carlton Winemakers Studio has helped make Carlton, Oregon, a popular destination for wine lovers. *Lisa D. Holmes.*

"That was when I first tasted great Pinot, and it was kind of mind-blowing. So that's what got me started thinking about Pinot noir, and it just stayed with me."

Fast-forward to college, where Eric was studying biochemistry with a general plan to work in medicine. He still liked wine, but he was getting serious about choosing a career, and medicine seemed like a responsible way to go. It was then that his high school "crush" resurfaced.

"It sounds strange based on the fact I was thinking about a career in medicine, but I officially realized I wanted to make wine when I was a freshman in college. I had an opportunity to go work a wine harvest…I think it was in '85. I stayed with a friend of the family who lived near Sonoma, and my first day of harvest was at Glen Ellen winery. This was when the Benzigers were just a little family thing. I loved everything about it. It was incredible. I left that day kind of electrified. And after doing it for the next several weeks, I was really just taken by it."

He continues, "So I went back to school thinking hard about winemaking, but I just couldn't get my head around switching to enology and viticulture. I mean wine chemistry just sounded like too much fun.

HAMACHER WINES

Hamacher Wines are made at the Carlton Winemakers Studio. CWS is an innovative, "green" cooperative winemaking facility that is an archetype for Oregon's wine industry and is the first of its kind built from the ground up in the nation. The fifteen-thousand-square-foot, gravity-flow winery, located on two acres in historic Carlton, has been home to some of the region's most exciting producers since 2002. The studio was specifically designed for multiple, small, premium wine producers in the Willamette Valley. It is home to nearly fourteen artisanal wineries. Each winery operates completely independent from one another. While there are separate cellars and staff, everyone benefits economically from state-of-the-art equipment.

YEAR FOUNDED: *1995*
OWNER: *Eric Hamacher*
WINEMAKER: *Eric Hamacher*
VARIETALS: *Pinot noir, Chardonnay*

TASTING ROOM LOCATION:
Carlton Winemakers Studio, 801 North Scott Street, Carlton, OR, 97111

HOURS: *open daily, 11:00 a.m.–5:00 p.m.*
FEE: *$10–$15*
CONTACT: *(503) 852-6100; jeff@winemakersstudio.com*

SUSTAINABILITY FEATURES:
- *LEED-designed facility*
- *high-efficiency process systems*
- *clear roofing materials*
- *day lighting, windows, doors, hallway*
- *night air cooling / CO_2 exhausting*
- *numerous additional sustainable design features*

In spite of my misgivings, I did end up applying to Davis to go into their biochem program, and I got in. But I wavered and pulled the rip cord at the last second and stayed in Southern California. But then the next year I came to terms with what I wanted to do. I once again applied to the enology program and made the move."

Practical Passion

Wine won the career battle and got Eric to UC–Davis, but he wasn't prepared to jettison his thoughtful and practical nature for any purely emotional bacchanal pursuits. So Eric decided to combine his studies in enology and viticulture with the more engineering-oriented programs in brewing and food science. This approach gave him a wider spectrum of influences from which to draw as he developed his understanding of how the winemaking process could work.

Food service (which Eric refers to as "canning tomatoes") didn't stand a chance, but he did well in brewing. In fact, his first job offer after school came from Anheuser-Busch. And although he had no real interest in a brewing career, his appreciation for its operational efficiencies helped Eric immensely in the next stage of his career.

In 1987, when Eric was still in school, he made his first trip to Oregon. A roommate at Davis who had grown up in the Willamette Valley brought some local Pinot noir down to show Eric what was happening here.

"I had never tasted anything like that from the New World. Quite frankly, it reminded me somewhat of wines I had tasted from Burgundy. And making Pinot was still my goal, so I figured I'd better get up here and find out what was going on. When I came up for that first harvest, I was here for about six months and got to know a lot of people here and fell in love with the place. So when I went home, I basically announced to my parents that I was going to live in Oregon. But then I had to figure out how to get moved up here and make it all happen, and that took another eight years."

CARLTON WINEMAKERS STUDIO

The Carlton Winemakers Studio is home to twelve individual vintners that produce some of the region's most coveted wines under one innovative roof. Located in the charming wine village of Carlton, it invites everyone to visit its state-of-the-art tasting room where you can taste its wines and learn about the unique stories behind each label.

YEAR FOUNDED: *2006*
OWNERS: *Eric Hamacher, Luisa Ponzi, Ned and Kirsten Lumpkin*
WINEMAKERS: *Andrew Rich, Bachelder, Dukes, Hamacher, Lazy River, Merriman, Montebruno, Omero, Retour, Trout Lily, Utopia, Wahle*

TASTING ROOM LOCATION:
801 North Scott Street, Carlton, OR, 97111

HOURS: *open daily, 11:00 a.m.–5:00 p.m.*
FEE: *$10–$15*
CONTACT: *(503) 852-6100; jeff@winemakersstudio.com*

LAYING THE GROUNDWORK

Throughout the early '90s, while working as a winemaker in California and in anticipation of his final move from Napa to Oregon in 1995, Eric acquired leases to a variety of vineyards throughout the northern Willamette Valley. This process gave him the material he would need to produce his first vintage, but it also meant that he would be blending a variety of wines, which was a far different approach than the increasingly popular move toward single-vineyard wines.

"As I was looking for the right place to hang my shingle, so to speak, I ended up with little bits of vineyards from all over, which I feel turned out to my advantage. '95 was a pretty cool, wet year, and ultimately, I felt that the wine I made was better than many of the individual vineyard wines made that year, so I was kind of off to the races on the idea of blending."

He continues, "That in itself was quite different because the single-vineyard idea had really taken hold, and a lot of people were sort of chasing that, but my wine was very well received. And people were like, 'Who the hell is this? It's brand new, and it's a wet vintage and it's a guy from a hot area. What's he doing in Oregon.' My wine and I definitely generated some interest. And I haven't really looked back. I've always blended my wines. I keep them separate in the fermenter, farm each differently based on its elevation, soil and what its needs are."

What turned out to be more of a challenge than acquiring grapes that led to mind-blowing Pinot was finding a permanent, reliable space to make it.

BUILDING A PERMANENT HOME

Because Oregon's wine industry was still young, the laws weren't set up to accommodate a growing industry. In fact, it was technically illegal for one winemaker to set up shop inside another winery. So even if Eric had found an established winery that would allow him to use its facilities, he couldn't do it legally.

Of course, people actually did this all the time, but it was with a wink and a nod and a hope that no one would get busted. So Eric took it on himself to get the law changed. It took three years of working with the Oregon legislature to accomplish that, but he got it done, to the great benefit of the state's economy and its many young winemakers. But legality is not the same thing as security.

Knowing that working in the corner of someone else's operation is a way to get by but not a long-term solution, Eric began to envision a new type of winery that would house a group of small winemakers that shared the space and the equipment. And in 2002, along with partners Ned and Kirsten Lumpkin of Lazy River Vineyard and his wife, Luisa Ponzi, Eric founded the Carlton Winemakers Studio, the first multiple winery facility to be built in Oregon.

"I think a lot of folks thought that there was no way the studio was going to work out because there were too many strong minds in one place—all of them certain that their grapes were the most important thing going through the property. And, you know, we had to do some things differently. We really

The Carlton Winemakers Studio currently is home to twelve wineries. *Lisa D. Holmes.*

looked at efficiency to make up for lack of space and really thought of it more as a processing center than a traditional winery."

He continues, "For example, a typical twenty-thousand-case facility in Oregon might do twenty tons a day, and that's with someone staying until the next morning. We're a twenty-five-thousand-case facility, and our biggest day so far was eighty-three tons and that was done in close to twelve hours. It's our efficiency—and the quality of our staff—that makes the idea of multiple wineries really feasible."

Since it began, the Carlton Winemakers Studio has served the needs of a number of different winemakers. Some have stayed with it, while others have outgrown it and moved on.

Eric Hamacher and his partners chose historic Carlton, Oregon, as the site for their winemaker incubator. *Lisa D. Holmes.*

"For some people—Penner-Ash, Soter, Scott Paul—they started here and kind of filled the pipe and then built their own facility. For others—Andrew Rich, myself, Lazy River—we're here, and who knows if we'll ever leave. Because it works. The biggest thing for us is, we have twelve wineries at the studio, all of them need to feel that their needs are being met, and so having a really strong staff that can organize twelve winemakers is kind of what makes it happen."

A Dream Realized

"It altogether feels like I've made some really good choices, and things are working out well. Without a doubt, Oregon was the right place. And you know, historically speaking, we're not that old as an industry here. I mean it's pretty magical that we still have many of the pioneers who started here…

they're still around. They're still part of the scene and people you can talk to and go to, and that feels really incredible."

He continues, "Plus, I love everything about making wine. I love that you're bottling a moment of time in the life of a piece of land. I love using traditional methods and doing as little as possible to influence the wine but understanding the chemistry behind that decision. And there's an intellectual side to wine that reflects the personalities of the people making it, at least on the level of wine that we're making in Oregon."

He concludes, "Most of all, I love the idea of breaking down the inhibitions that we have as people. It's hard to not share with someone sitting across the table when there's a bottle of wine between you."—JV

Chapter 10

THIBAUD MANDET

PIONEER IN THE NEW WORLD

This book was inspired during a time when I was selling French wine barrels to Oregon winemakers. Twice each year, the owner of the cooperage would visit from France, and I would schedule meetings for us with winemakers in their cellars. We would travel to wineries and taste maturing wines drawn from barrels through a thief. Most of the winemakers made time for us eventually because it was also a time to check their wines fermenting in barrels and hear firsthand about what was going on in other parts of the world from the cooperage owner, who spent all his time circling the globe, tasting wines in traditional venues of prominence but also in emerging wine regions in such places as Vietnam and China. I would listen to the analytical wine banter and the funny stories, taste and spit with them.

Among the winemakers I was unable to meet despite my outreach efforts was Thibaud Mandet of WillaKenzie Estate. Anytime I called on Thibaud, it seemed he was bottling! In fact, I recall an unscheduled stop one afternoon at the overwhelmingly beautiful WillaKenzie vineyard and hearing the bottling machine clanking somewhere down the hill. The tasting room attendant told us Thibaud was bottling and telephoned him to come up for a short visit, but he politely declined. It makes sense to me now. I began our interview by asking him why all the bottling? I didn't hear this from other winemakers.

"If I say I love to bottle, it would be a lie," said Thibaud, a Frenchman and WillaKenzie's winemaker for eleven years. "It is hard and redundant, but I learn to appreciate it because it is a very important step of winemaking;

Above: For WillaKenzie Estate, the concept of terroir is so important that they named both their Yamhill estate and Dundee Hills vineyard after their soil types. *Lisa D. Holmes.*

Below: WillaKenzie Estate's guests are afforded spectacular views. *WillaKenzie Estate.*

you must control it just as well as planting, as well as all the processes of winemaking, until you put your baby in the bottle."

WillaKenzie Estate comprises 420 acres—130 acres of hillside are farmed and managed by the estate, which produces roughly twenty thousand cases of wine annually. The majority, 70 percent, is Pinot noir. Pinot gris accounts for another 18 percent. The remaining acreage is divided between Pinot blanc, Gamay noir, Pinot meunier and a little Chardonnay.

The manageable size of the vineyard affords Thibaud tight control over all aspects of wine production, and he routinely performs physical duties such as racking and filling barrels and working in the vineyard tasting and sampling grapes. He enjoys the physical labor of winemaking, but he also feels that if he does it himself on occasion, he will be better suited to direct others in best practices. "I like the combination of hard work and blending. I love to be at every step of the winemaking. To make sure that you can do the job well," he said.

For example, Thibaud bottles wine every four to five months, and routinely running the bottling machine also helps maintain it. "If you use it one time a year, it is like leaving your car sitting in the garage. You will have some problems with the cables and gaskets," Thibaud said.

Thibaud hails from Auvergne, France, a region in the center of France. He comes from a family of doctors who dabbled in winemaking and, on his mother's side, had a farm. As a child, he was, now and again, offered "just a very tiny little bit" of wine from his parents. As such, he developed a discerning palate and confidence in his ability to detect a good wine. After an undergraduate degree in chemistry, Thibaud decided that winemaking would be his career. His family was overjoyed. He received his graduate diploma from Bordeaux's famed Faculté d'Oenologie de Bordeaux. Afterward, he obtained a postgraduate degree in sparkling winemaking from Reims in Champagne.

It is important to impart that France produces the most heralded wines in the world. The tradition stems back to ancient times. Bordeaux, where Thibaud studied winemaking, is the largest wine-growing region in France, and average vintages produce more than 700 million bottles of wine, which range from table wine to some of the most desired wines in the world.

Bordeaux wine is produced by roughly 8,500 concerns. Conversely, Oregon has 592 producers, according to the American Winery Guide. Burgundy, France, is an internationally acclaimed wine-producing area well known for Pinot noir and Chardonnay wines. The region is heralded for quality wine often produced in small quantities. Burgundy vineyards are mainly planted on the hillsides.

WILLAKENZIE ESTATE

Passion for Pinot with a "Sense of Place" is what defines WillaKenzie Estate, a family-owned boutique winery located in the heart of the Willamette Valley in Oregon. It produces Pinot noir, Pinot blanc, Pinot gris and small amounts of Pinot meunier, Gamay noir and Chardonnay. Its wines are made from grapes sustainably grown on the estate and their old-world style reflects the winery's French heritage. WillaKenzie Estate represents Oregon terroir at its best.

OWNERS: *Bernard and Ronni Lacroute*
WINEMAKER: *Thibaud Mandet*
VARIETALS: *Pinot noir, Pinot meunier, Pinot blanc, Pinot gris, Gamay noir, Chardonnay*

TASTING ROOM LOCATION:
19143 Laughlin Road, Yamhill, OR, 97148

HOURS: *open daily, 10:00 a.m.–5:00 p.m. May–November; 10:00 a.m.–4:00 p.m. November–April*

FEE: *$20*
CONTACT: *(503) 662-3280; tastepinot@willakenzie.com*

VINEYARDS:
* *WillaKenzie Estate Vineyards (Yamhill/Carlton AVA)*
* *Jory Hills Vineyards (Dundee Hills AVA)*

Thibaud's view of Oregon is that it is the New World, an open frontier for winemaking with a world-class growing climate. It is also a place that affords a winemaker tremendous flexibility, control and an opportunity to build and innovate. In contrast, Burgundy's traditions stem back thousands of years, and all the land suitable for grape growing is already planted. "They are sustaining what is already there," Thibaud said. "To be part of this great project of exploring new terroir and learning with the age of the vines is very exciting."

Oregon has wet, mild winters, a long growing season and comparatively low risk of vineyard disease, thunderstorms and hailstorms, which can damage the grapes. Another positive attribute is the Willamette Valley's proximity to the comparatively stable Pacific Ocean. Burgundy is affected by the more volatile Atlantic Ocean. "We can feel lucky to have such stability in the weather," he said. "Fair to say, I love my country, and in Burgundy, they are making wonderful wines that I love."

Thibaud quickly added that he spends a lot of time enjoying wines from all over the world, comparing and looking for ways to improve his wines. "It is very important to learn what you can and not spend all my time with my own wine."

Thibaud came to Oregon in 2000. He saw a job posting for a harvest internship at WillaKenzie on the job board in the main hall of his university in Bordeaux. He quickly reached out to then winemaker Laurent, a Frenchman, who was looking for someone to help with the harvest but also someone with a chemistry background to do a little research in the laboratory.

Thibaud learned that the owner of WillaKenzie, Bernard Lacroute, was also French originally from Burgundy and made his home in the United States forty years ago. Laurent told Thibaud that it would only be for a few months and that if he did well, he might have an opportunity to stay. For a fledgling winemaker, an internship is similar to winning a scholarship

Thibaud's first internship was in 1998 at a massive winery in the high desert of Texas. "Don't mess with Texas," Thibaud quipped. He spent nine months and two harvests at the winery. It was a "crazy project that the French and the Texans owned one thousand acres together." The vineyard produced moderately priced wines in large volumes. Thibaud learned a lot during those stints and fell in love with the people of Texas.

"People thought I was very funny because they have not seen a lot of French over there. It was a very special experience. They did greet me very nicely."

The experience was invaluable, as he learned about the financial and logistical demands of a large winery. Thibaud reflects on those times and feels grateful. "I don't think you are born or trained to be a good winemaker. You become one after several successful harvests," he said, adding that many people do not get that chance. "There are a lot of people that are sometimes stuck in the lab or working in sales."

The mass-quantity experience of the Texan winery is a stark contrast to the boutique atmosphere at WillaKenzie, where quality is paramount, and Thibaud has a direct hand in every aspect of the wine's evolution.

WillaKenzie Estate is situated in the rolling hills near Yamhill, Oregon. *WillaKenzie Estate.*

After his successful internship at WillaKenzie, Thibaud was elated with the invitation to stay on. And in 2003, another opening occurred for winemaker. Thibaud interviewed for the job along with many outsiders and was afforded the opportunity.

"It was a big challenge for me, I have to be honest. You ask yourself, 'Am I going to be able to do that?' Because you are in charge. If the wine is bad, it is your fault. You cannot hide yourself behind someone and say, 'He told me so.'"

As winemaker, Thibaud learned at an even faster rate. Today, after eleven years as winemaker, he continues to learn and build on his experiences. In fact, starting a new vintage is profoundly exciting to him to a point that he welcomes aging. "The beauty of knowing you are getting older is you are wiser," he said.

Thibaud shifted his focus to customer perceptions and the reality of working at a winery. "I don't want to break their dreams, but it is important to tell people there is a tremendous amount of hours in the vineyard and winery," he said. "There is a lot of sweat and hard work. It is not always sunny and beautiful weather, and the rain, the winters and springs are very tough here in Oregon as opposed to California."

Thibaud said that he understands the need for a face to represent the winery and that it makes sense to have the winemaker play this role. He also feels that there are many anonymous contributors whose hard work directly affects the fineness of the final product. "It is good that the winemaker takes some credit, but it is teamwork—people of the vineyard and winery are doing the work too," he said. "It is not sitting on the chair in the lab having fun tasting things. Yes, this is fun, but there is also a lot of moving barrels and making sure the wine is being taken care of."

The winemaker's blending decisions are vastly important, but the magic is in the quality of what the winemaker has to work with. "I got lucky to work for a company respectful of growing high-quality vineyards," he said. "If I have crazy ideas [in blending], I can make something bad, but I can not make a good wine from a bad harvest or a mediocre vineyard."

Thibaud enjoys the sense of community in Oregon, as do others. He shared that it has been uplifting to be a part of the tight-knit Oregon wine community where everyone promotes the state's brand. "We are down to earth and grounded. We want to make a profit, but there is a lot of friendships and respect among the winemakers. That makes me feel good to be part of that. We can all succeed that way."—VP

Chapter 11

KELLEY FOX

ALLOWING WINE TO EXPRESS ITS NATURE

K elley Fox waved from behind the glass wall when she saw me standing in the outer equipment room of the Scott Paul winery in Carlton, Oregon. She was in with the barrels, and even though it was early in the day, she was moving with purpose—clearly in control. And that's just how Kelley likes it.

To hear her tell it, she has lived her life dividing her time between proving other people wrong and jumping into her latest passion with both feet. But regardless, it's always on her terms, and she always is in control of her own destiny. When she stops to talk, she's very clear about the fact that she makes wines that are natural, and she goes to great length to explain what that really means. But I'm jumping too far ahead. Let's get back to the beginning, in Europe. Holland, to be precise.

The European Influence

When Kelley was four years old, her still very young parents (they were nineteen and twenty-one when she was born) moved from the American Midwest to The Hague, which is the third-largest city in the Netherlands and where Kelley lived until she was eleven.

These early years in Holland shaped Kelley's sensibilities in a way the United States simply couldn't. And when she recalls what it was like growing

Scott Paul Wines is dedicated to Pinot noir, both the wines created by winemaker Kelley Fox and the wines they import from France's Burgundy wine region. *Scott Paul Wines.*

up, she oozes romanticism. "The feeling there was just so different from here. There were no strip malls or billboards. It was a city, but it was stone and mist and sea air; our gardener with wooden shoes; our garden wall. The North Sea was so powerful that if we didn't have that wall, your hair would probably blow off. I spoke fluent Dutch. The people there thought my brother and I both were Dutch."

She continues, "When my mom cooked, what would happen is the fisherman would come on his bike and knock on our door. She would go out to the street, and he'd open his wooden box on the front of his bike and show her the fish he caught. She'd choose the fish, and he would filet it on white paper on top of the box. And that's often how we ate. I grew up with milk coming in glass and being delivered to the door. Bread ladies with hot breads came by, or when we bought things out, there was a baker and a butcher and everything separate, you know, not everything at the store. All these things, and then, of course, our travels."

Kelley remembers going to Majorca often. Her parents were young and didn't hesitate to take their kids to parties or other social gatherings. Those are her memories of Europe—parties, outings, swans, parks, rain, the North Sea. Very wholesome. And wine was a part of that, so she learned to view wine as a wholesome thing.

But Kelley's time in Europe also was the time when her more willful and rebellious side began to show through. "My brother and I were forbidden to go to a woods near our home, so naturally that's where we spent a lot of our time. It was beautiful, and it was wild. I believe that's how we all should be." This helps to explain some of her discomfort with the Dallas prep school that soon followed.

SCOTT PAUL WINES

The winery, located in downtown Carlton, is housed in a repurposed granary built in 1900, while the brick tasting room was originally a creamery, built in 1915. Today, the winery uses this space to craft Pinot noirs of elegance and finesse by adhering to the centuries-old essentials of old vines, low yields and meticulous, minimal winemaking Grapes and must are moved only by gravity. Fermentation is conducted only by wild, indigenous yeasts. Malolactic fermentation is allowed to occur naturally. The Burgundian techniques of Pigeage (punch-down) and Remontage (pump-over) are used as means of gentle extraction. French oak barrels (less than 20 percent new) are used to age the wines—to let them breathe and mature.

YEAR FOUNDED: *1999*
OWNERS: *Martha and Scott Wright; Cameron Healy and Suzy Snow*
WINEMAKER: *Kelley Fox*
VARIETALS: *Pinot noir*

TASTING ROOM LOCATION AND HOURS:

In Wine Country: *winery and tasting room—128 South Pine Street, Carlton, OR, 97111*
    Open to the public for tastings Saturdays, noon–5:00 p.m.
    Open for tastings by appointment Tuesday–Friday, noon–5:00 p.m. (reserve ahead)
    Open for wine shopping Tuesday–Friday, noon–5:00 p.m.

In Portland: *urban loft tasting room—2537 Northwest Upshur Street, Portland, OR, 97210*
    Open to the public for tastings Fridays, 5:00 p.m.–8:00 p.m.

TASTING FEE: *$10*
CONTACT: *(503) 852-7300; kellykarr@scottpaul.com*

SUSTAINABILITY FEATURES:
- *biodynamic farming*
- *wind power*
- *tree-free paper for labels*
- *repurposed buildings for winery and tasting room*

SENTENCED TO PREP SCHOOL

As a result of what would probably be labeled precociousness, soon after her family moved back to the United States from Holland, Kelley found herself in the very tony Hockaday School in Dallas, Texas.

"I'm not of that club, you know. I mean, I did well with my grades, but I was always one of those kids who never lived up to my potential. I look back now and suppose I was that way on purpose. I resisted everything just by instinct. I understand now that it's just something that comes from inside me."

But at that time, she only knew she didn't really fit. Especially when the time came to choose a college. "My family wasn't well off like a lot of those girls' families. We couldn't afford Cornell or Princeton or what have you, so I did what I thought was probably the worst thing I could do at that time…I went to Texas A&M to become a vet."

In fact, Kelley had two goals in her early life. One was to be a fine artist like her mother, and the other was to be a veterinarian. Unfortunately, the veterinarian scheme didn't go as planned, so she ended up getting a liberal arts degree, which featured studies in psychology, English literature and folk medicine. Which of those three is not like the others? If you answered folk medicine, you get the prize, and Kelley gets a career direction.

Strange as it may sound, Kelley had become enamored of the idea of moving to equatorial regions to study botanical medicines, and that brought her to Oregon. Well, it was that combined with a career counselor who told her she could never, ever, ever succeed in science. It only seems natural that she would interpret that advice as a good reason to become a biochemist.

HELLO OREGON STATE

For a budding biochemist who had no money and had never even visited Oregon, Oregon State seemed to be the perfect location to begin her adventure. Why? Because OSU was ranked as one of the top twenty-five schools in the country in biochemistry and because the weather in western Oregon—if you think about it—is a lot like the weather in The Hague.

"I packed all my shit and moved to Oregon. Never been here in my life, had no prospects, no job, no contacts, no house and I was broke. So

KELLEY FOX WINES

Kelley Fox, the winemaker at Scott Paul Wines, created her own label—Kelley Fox Wines—in 2007, along with her father, Gerson Stearns. She brings thirteen years (and counting) experience as a winemaker, from stints at Tori Mor, Hamacher and Eyrie, where she worked with her mentor, David Lett. Her annual case production ranges from one hundred to six hundred cases. The first vintage was 2007. She makes three wines: the Maresh Vineyard Pinot Noir, the Momtazi Vineyard Pinot Noir and the Mirabai Pinot Noir. The wines are made in Carlton, Oregon.

YEAR FOUNDED: *2007*
OWNER: *Kelley Fox*
WINEMAKER: *Kelley Fox*
VARIETALS: *Pint noir*

TASTING ROOM LOCATION: *none*
CONTACT: *(503) 679-5786; kelley@kelleyfoxwines.com*

SUSTAINABILITY FEATURES:
- *Demeter-certified biodynamic vineyard (Momtazi Vineyard)*
- *organic and biodynamically farmed (Maresh Vineyard)*

my intention was to live here for a year and get residency, then enter the program. I lived in a little town called Alsea, which basically is a town of 465…many of whom at that time were gingered loggers."

Needless to say, Kelley's doublewide on the Alsea River was a big change from Dallas. But after weathering some fairly extreme culture shock, Kelley eventually started going to school and ended up loving it, particularly quantum physics. She earned graduate degrees in biochemistry and biophysics. But it was her work isolating enzymes in pig brains that did two very important things. It taught her that she could be successful doing scientific work, and it helped her understand that she needed a different career.

"After a while, I just started telling myself that there's got to be something else. And then I met someone planting a vineyard, and that person ended up

Scott Paul's brick tasting room in Carlton, Oregon, was originally a creamery, built in 1915. *Lisa D. Holmes.*

being the father of my two children. And he kept saying, 'Kelley, you should be a winemaker. You really should.'"

EVERYTHING FALLS INTO PLACE

"I grew up with wine. My parents still drink wine every day with their meals. I mean, I've always loved wine, but I'd never really thought that much about it. But right then, at that point in time, something just clicked in me, and I went from zero to 100 percent and became a winemaker. And it's been 100 percent ever since."

Once she made the decision to leap wholeheartedly into winemaking, Kelley managed to land some remarkable opportunities. She was part of the winemaking team at Hamacher Wines and was winemaker/general manager at Torii Mor—both respected Oregon wineries. And, of course, her work alongside legendary Oregon wine industry pioneer David Lett at Eyrie Vineyards helped her become the winemaker she is today.

But nobody should think even for a moment that anyone besides Kelley herself really defines her as a winemaker. She does what she does because she feels she has to. She has functioned this way her entire life, and there's no changing things now. She gives herself to it completely. She does it for love.

In fact, it's the love she feels for the land, the vines, the grapes, the whole cycle of life, really, that guides Kelley's effort to allow the wine she makes to express its true nature.

Scott Paul Wines also repurposed its winery, which originally was the Madsen Grain Company, built in 1900. *Lisa D. Holmes.*

"It takes great courage to allow the wine to be naked. To allow these plants on a particular piece of land to truly express themselves. Each wine tells a story…of the year, the land, the vines and also what happens in the winery. Each winemaker guides that process—you do it in your own way—and you are reflected in the wine, but you do not make the wine. You allow the wine to become what it truly is."

KEEPING IT NATURAL

Kelley goes to some length to convey how committed she is to allowing a wine to reflect the season and the land, but keeping it natural doesn't mean you can just ignore the person who will end up drinking the wine.

"I believe it's important to allow a wine to express its nature, but this is not to say you just let the wine take its own course. It's not even close to that. I want my wines to express themselves, but there's no excuse for them not being sound and enjoyable in the glass. If it doesn't give you pleasure, I mean, who's going to buy fifty dollars worth of principle? I'm not. I can't afford it. No one wants that."

She adds, "You want to have a companion that's pleasurable, that doesn't need a lot of attention, that doesn't compete with your blood/brain barrier and your food. I mean, it doesn't have to be a bomb of pleasure, right? But something that quietly flows into your meal or into your time talking with friends. A wine that will settle itself into your company and give you charm…That's all I ask."—JV

Chapter 12

ANNA MATZINGER AND
MICHAEL DAVIES

FROM HARVEST GLOBE-TROTTERS TO VINTNERS
WITH ROOTS IN OREGON

Anna Matzinger and Michael Davies met in 1998 while working a grape harvest in California. I suppose this could be viewed as an unlikely meeting spot for a young woman from Idaho and a young man from New Zealand. But the travel that brings people together from faraway places is simply part of the wine world, and it was their love of travel that helped lead Anna and Michael to wine in the first place.

After finishing college, both Anna and Michael began traveling the world, which is not always easy when one is young and without means. So, it makes sense that they would gravitate to the grapes as a means to that end.

"Anna and I discovered early on that the wine industry is very encouraging of travel. We both had traveled a lot prior…outside the wine industry, but once we got started working with wine, we realized how great it was to travel to a new part of the world, meet a whole new group of people—and not just in a momentary sense as you might in a youth or backpackers hostel—but work alongside them for six to twelve weeks and really get to know them. And that's what we were doing when we met…working harvest in Dry Creek Valley in Sonoma County. But in different wineries."

Anna adds, "Michael was working at a winery called Lambert Bridge, and I was at a lovely location called Preston. We had to work hard, but we saw each other occasionally and obviously hit it off. Anyway, after that, I was heading back to an assistant winemaker job in Hunter Valley in Australia, and I thought Michael should come. Honestly, the thought occurred to me that he was going to go to the airport and fly home, and I'd never see him again. So, I

An at-home blending session for Matzinger Davies Wine Company. *Anna Matzinger.*

convinced him to come work the vintage in Australia, which was before his next job started in New Zealand. That meant he had enough time to spend several weeks with me in Australia before his next harvest commitment."

And with that, we have some inkling of how Anna and Michael thought about life at that point in time. Their world was attuned to the seasons and was defined by the grape-growing regions around the globe. But as they thought more about staying together, the way they approached their work began to change.

CONSOLIDATING A VISION

Anna and Michael did work together that next harvest in Australia, which created a variety of interesting challenges and ended with Anna not being able to get her permanent work visa. So she followed Michael to New Zealand. And that's when their seasonal work plans came to an end.

Michael sets the stage for us. "As I said earlier, the wine industry is so forgiving and appealing because of the travel, but there's a kind of boom and bust to

Matzinger Davies' Sauvignon blanc bottling line. *Michael Davies.*

it. When harvest ends and you go into winter, the amount of work drops, and people's morale tends to reflect that. So there we were in Marlborough, needing to find our next fix."

"Michael found his. He landed a job in Spain, but I didn't."

"And that's when we both kind of had a sense that Oregon might be a good target. We both knew people who had worked here, and Anna even knew people who lived here."

Anna had met Cheryl Francis, now an owner at REX HILL, through a college friend when Cheryl was making wine at Chehalem winery, which happens to be located across the road from REX HILL, the current home of Matzinger Davies wines.

"I contacted Cheryl and asked if they needed anyone, which they did. And Michael kindly made the decision to come to Oregon with me rather than go off to Spain. So, we came to Oregon planning to be here for three or four months before moving on to Chile or figuring something else out for Europe. But by the end of that harvest in '99, we both had been offered permanent jobs that we felt were too good to walk away from. So we're still here."

ESTABLISHING A RECORD OF SUCCESS

Both Anna and Michael can speak to the seductiveness of following the harvest—the energy and romance can be exhilarating. But they also both agree that the tough transition that must be made to build a successful career in winemaking is selecting the right permanent job and then proving yourself.

As Michael puts it, "To really progress in your learning, you've got to stay somewhere all the way through from fruit to the wine in the bottle and then watch what happens from there." And surprisingly, they both believed that they had found jobs worth pursuing in the same place at the same time.

Anna and Michael spent the first few years in Oregon living at Chehalem winery with Harry Peterson-Nedry, Chehalem's owner. But it was Michael who ended up working at Chehalem, first as cellar master and vineyard manager and then as assistant winemaker. Eventually, Michael would move on to become winemaker at REX HILL, the position he holds today.

And instead of working at Chehalem as she thought she would, Anna was offered the job of assistant winemaker to Sam Tannahill at Archery Summit. Tannahill is now married to Cheryl Francis and a co-owner of REX HILL.

After a few years at Archery Summit, Anna moved into the winemaker position. By that time, she clearly had learned how to create a memorable wine. In fact, one of Anna's wines—Archery Summit Estate Pinot Noir 2004—was chosen to be paired with the main course at the first State Dinner in President Obama's White House. But to hear her tell it, making really good wine is a process that never really ends.

"When I was first promoted to winemaker at Archery Summit, I thought there were all these right answers and that I just needed to know what the right answer was. But I think the more I did it, the more I felt comfortable with my own intuition and the idea that maybe there isn't a right answer, or perhaps more accurately, there are many right answers. I believe that level of understanding comes with experience, comes with confidence, comes with trial and error."

Michael agrees. "It's personal. The right answer depends on who you are and what you're trying to do. And it takes time to figure that out." So, this pair of winemakers settled down, continued to hone their skills and gave up their seasonal journeys.

MAKING A HOME

After spending time plying their craft at separate wineries, though, Anna and Michael realized that they wanted to do what was probably viewed as inevitable to those around them. They wanted their own label. And out of that desire, Matzinger Davies Wines was born, although according to Michael, they were never in a rush to get there.

"I don't think we were in a hurry to start our own label. Just like with kids…we weren't in a hurry to have kids, even though we knew deep down that we intended to. It was the same with our own wine label. But in 2006, we

MATZINGER DAVIES WINE COMPANY

The Matzinger Davies Wine Company is a collaboration between husband and wife winemakers Michael Davies and Anna Matzinger. It all started with that powerful idea "let's make something together" and came to fruition in 2006 with their first vintage of Pinot noir and Chardonnay. Coincidentally, that was the same year as the birth of their first child. Their Pinot noir comes from two small vineyards in the Eola-Amity Hills AVA. Each vineyard is farmed with dedication and affection by their respective owners, who live on site. The Chardonnay represents a journey of exploration and discovery, employing fruit from a different site or AVA each year. They also produce a small amount of Sauvignon blanc from the Columbia River Gorge (Michael is a New Zealander by birth, which should explain this). The intention of Matzinger Davies Wine Company is to produce wines with a resonant voice, speaking to geographical origin, varietal typicity and season. Authenticity, vibrancy and integrity should be their calling cards.

YEAR FOUNDED: *2006*
OWNERS: *Anna Matzinger and Michael Davies*
WINEMAKERS: *Anna Matzinger and Michael Davies*
VARIETALS: *Pinot noir, Sauvignon blanc, Chardonnay, Grenache*

TASTING ROOM LOCATION:
None. Wines available at REX HILL.

CONTACT: *(503) 437-0155; anna@matzingerdavies.com*

committed to some fruit and made the wine, and that was our first vintage. And we've been doing it ever since."

Anna points out that there was a lot going on that summer, and that their first wine together was not even the biggest highlight. "We made the decision to get married in 2005, and in 2006, our son was born. So '06 saw the birth of many possibilities."

In addition to a son and a new label, 2006 was the year Michael joined REX HILL and A to Z wineries. It's at REX HILL where Anna and Michael have continued to make their own wine. And since leaving Archery Summit

REX HILL winery, home to REX HILL and A to Z Wineworks. *REX HILL.*

in early 2013 as winemaker and co–general manager, Anna now can focus more fully on the Matzinger Davies label.

"They've been amazingly accommodating of our personal label," says Michael of REX HILL's owners. "Rather than simply tolerate it, they've embraced it and even featured it in their tasting room. And we are deeply appreciative of that."

So, did they make the right decision to abandon their global wandering and settle in Oregon's Willamette Valley? They believe so. Anna tells us why. "Professionally, it's a great place to make Pinot noir. But there's another part to that. On a personal level, this is simply a great place to be. The wine community is singular. It's interesting. It's different from other places where I've worked. It is a really terrific community, and I think while the jobs are important, it's the community that's kept us here. It's a great place to live and raise your family. And I think that's important. Not only for the people who work in this industry but the larger narrative about this being a place where world-class wine is made."

Michael agrees and adds some perspective. "From a historical standpoint, it seems like the winemakers who came in right after the pioneers got started

REX HILL

REX HILL has been making elegant Pinot noirs for more than thirty years in Oregon's Willamette Valley. The landmark winery and biodynamic vineyards are located just outside Newberg at the gateway to Oregon's Willamette Valley wine country, and visitors are welcome daily to taste and explore. All the fruit for REX HILL wines is hand-picked and hand-sorted, and wines are hand-made in small fermenters and barrels. REX HILL has an extensive wine library, including large formats, and offers entertaining wine classes, harvest tours and club events.

YEAR FOUNDED: *1982*
OWNERS: *Bill Hatcher, Deb Hatcher, Sam Tannahill, Cheryl Francis*
WINEMAKER: *Michael Davies*
VARIETALS: *Pinot noir, Chardonnay*

TASTING ROOM LOCATION:
30835 North Highway 99W, Newberg, OR, 97132

HOURS: *open daily, 10:00 a.m.–5:00 p.m.*
FEE: *$10*
CONTACT: *(800) 739-4455; info@REXHILL.com*

SUSTAINABILITY FEATURES:
* *all estate vineyards farmed bio-dynamically, organically or LIVE standards*

really had a lot to do with setting the tone of how the winemaking community here should collaborate. How everyone could gain by working together…the 'all ships rise with the rising tide' mentality. And that still carries through today. It's remained a fundamental value within this community. It may not last forever, but it's probably one of the most important reasons why we chose to settle here in Oregon."—JV

Chapter 13

ANTHONY KING

HUMBLE, EASYGOING AND MASTERFUL

If Anthony King had not previously realized how important wine had become to him, it surely came clear the day his wife handed him a journal and said, "Please. Just write it down and stop talking to me about wine." So he did. He journaled about wine, as well as about all the ways wine was beginning to take over his life.

At the time, Anthony and his wife lived in Austin, Texas. Not a place one normally thinks of when the subject of wine comes up. But there was enough going on with wine to completely capture Anthony's attention.

"I had taken some classes from a local sommelier, and then I started hanging around a wine shop called the Austin Wine Merchant. In fact, I did that so much, the owner, John Rennick, said, 'Hey, do you want to work here, because you're here all the time anyway.' So I started working there, and by that time, I was in maybe four tasting groups. I think I was starting to annoy some of my friends who didn't really care that much about wine."

Based on his wife's reaction, it appears that Anthony was annoying more people than he realized. But as he has risen in the wine world, he's never had a stronger supporter than the woman who helped him focus his thoughts. And the journey has been a fascinating one.

GETTING HIS FEET WET

The winemaking part of Anthony's journey didn't get off to the smoothest start. He first tried making wine at home. And he failed. Miserably.

So he tried another tack. Anthony went to work for a guy everyone told him was the best winemaker around. A guy named Jim Johnson, who happens to be one of the most respected winemakers in Texas.

For the next two seasons, Anthony helped Jim and his wife, Karen, wherever he could, sometimes waking at 4:00 a.m. to drive a few hours north to Johnson's vineyard and work for several hours and then drive back to work his regular day job as a physics textbook writer. He filled every moment with wine and food, eventually getting hired to write about wine for the *Austin Chronicle*. Finally, he became more serious about wine as a career and started taking classes with the goal of getting into UC–Davis.

Adding school to his full-time job, work in the vineyards, freelance work for the *Chronicle* and odd hours in the wine shop might seem exhausting to some people, but Anthony thought it was fun. Maybe that's because everything worked out in the end. Or maybe that's just how he is. I do know that when

Lemelson Vineyards winery makes a proud statement at sunset. *Lemelson Vineyards*.

LEMELSON VINEYARDS

Eric Lemelson planted 2 acres of Pinot noir as a hobby on a hillside farm near Newberg in 1995. He enjoyed viticulture so much that within two years he had planted 17 additional acres near Carlton and begun to design a winery. Today, Lemelson Vineyards owns and manages 156 acres at seven sites in three AVAs (Yamhill-Carlton, Dundee Hills and Chehalem Mountains) in Yamhill County. All vineyards have been farmed organically from the beginning and have been certified organic since 2004. The gravity-flow winery reflects both a strong commitment to sustainability, grounded in Eric Lemelson's background as an environmental lawyer, and a "no-compromises" approach to wine quality. Winemaker Anthony King crafts distinctive, ageworthy Pinot noir, Chardonnay, Riesling and Pinot gris.

YEAR FOUNDED: *1999*
OWNER: *Eric Lemelson*
WINEMAKER: *Anthony King*
VARIETALS: *Pinot noir, Chardonnay, Riesling, Pinot gris*

TASTING ROOM LOCATION:
12020 Northeast Stag Hollow Road, Carlton, OR, 97111

HOURS: *open daily, 11:00 a.m.–5:00 p.m.*
FEE: *$10*
CONTACT: *info@lemelsonvineyards.com*

SUSTAINABILITY FEATURES:
- *100 percent certified organic estate vineyards spread across the northern Willamette Valley*
- *50kW solar array*
- *founding member of the Oregon Carbon Neutral Challenge*
- *employee hybrid incentive program*

you talk to this tall, lanky, soft-spoken Texan, it seems like it would take a lot to ruffle his feathers.

Either way, at the end of his required coursework, Anthony and his wife were off to California to pursue the dream and begin working in a large Napa Valley winery that had offered Anthony a harvest job.

LEARNING THE BUSINESS

Working at Acacia in Napa's Carneros region was a different world than the small wineries near Austin.

"For the first few weeks of harvest, all I did was pump-overs all day. You know, where you pump the wine from the bottom of the tank to the top while it's fermenting. I'd do pump-overs for sixteen hours and then clean up my lines and go home, then come in the next day and start doing them again. And we had to do them fast. It didn't take long for all of us to get tired of it, and I started feeling kind of resentful towards my

Lemelson Vineyards features certified organic estate vineyards spread across the northern Willamette Valley. *Lisa D. Holmes.*

boss, Michael Terrien, until he did something that has informed how I try to work with people."

He continues, "I was up on a catwalk, and Michael walked up to me and asked how I was doing, and I said, 'Good' even though I was kind of pissed that I hadn't learned much other than how to run a pump. But then he told me how much he appreciated what I was doing and that I was doing a great job, and that little exchange sustained me for the next three days. Since then, I've always remembered to thank people for what they do."

In time, Anthony's diligence paid off; following harvest, he was hired as a lab tech. This happened at about the same time he failed to get into UC–Davis.

But fate (and diligence) managed to put the wheels back on the cart. Knowing Anthony wanted to enter the university's enology program, Michael talked to the people at Davis to let them know that they were missing an opportunity. So, when an applicant turned down his invitation to enter the program, Anthony got the call. He began studying winemaking at UC–Davis.

GROWING INTO THE ROLE

"My first year at Davis, I kept in touch with Michael. All my research was going to be based on my work at Acacia. All Pinot noir. So by the second year, he had hired me back on full time, and I did all of my research on full-sized Pinot noir fermentations at Acacia. And by the time I was out of school, I was assistant winemaker."

Anthony spent seven years at Acacia. He became part of the history of that winery as it continued to prove that good Pinot noir could be made in the Carneros AVA. But suddenly, when the winery was sold to international liquor conglomerate Diageo, everything changed completely.

"I had only been winemaker for a year when Diageo bought the winery, and Michael left for a position at Hanzell Winery in Sonoma. His departure left a gaping hole in the team, and I didn't even have an assistant winemaker to help me wade through the transition. Meanwhile, Diageo wanted to increase production from 90,000 cases a year to 180,000 cases a year. And obviously at that point, philosophy and quality go out the window; you're just trying to get it done."

He adds, "When it came down to it, I was miserable. I didn't like the corporate lifestyle, which is what I had tried to avoid most of my life. So I started looking for something else, and then I saw Eric Lemelson's ad, which said, 'Looking for a winemaker who wants to work in a non-corporate environment.' How perfect was that?"

HELLO, OREGON

Anthony called Eric Lemelson. He already was familiar with the Lemelson winery because of an article he had read about the facility's innovative engineering. In fact, when he was in Oregon for the 2005 International Pinot Noir Celebration (IPNC), he drove out to the facility to see its ingenious design but only got as far as the front gate.

"I drove up to the locked gate in '05 and looked around, hoping someone would open the door, but the tasting room didn't used to be open. It was just this giant building. No signs, except there was a Lemelson Vineyards sign on

Solar arrays attest to Lemelson Vineyards' commitment to sustainability. *Lisa D. Holmes.*

the gate so I knew I was in the right place. It's interesting that I ended up working here."

After an intriguing first conversation on the phone, Anthony met Eric for an interview in San Francisco. It was definitely a non-corporate experience.

"Eric was with his mom, his wife, their nanny and his son; that was the interview. We got along great, and then I flew up to see the place in person; I think that was in May 2006. I was sold and started that summer. And I've been here ever since, working with mostly the same people."

Anthony came in to a much smaller Willamette Valley winery from a very large California operation, but don't think he came in brimming with confidence and thinking that he was an amazing winemaker who was going to make his new operation a whole lot better. That's not his style. Plus, he knew he had risen in the ranks really fast. Instead, he employed what he refers to as his mother's ethics, which basically was to work really hard and through that work learn how to make things well and treat people with respect. And he always kept in mind how important it is to listen and to say thank you to the people who help you get where you need to go.

"We changed things slowly after I got here. The assistant winemaker and the vineyard manager who were already here showed me what had been done prior to my arrival. And then we'd talk through those processes. It always took a little longer to do things because you had to have conversations all the time. But finally we made changes and developed systems that made sense to everybody, and we continue to look for better ways of doing everything. For that reason, I like having good people come and work here because they bring good ideas. In the end, listening to those ideas is one way of becoming a better winemaker."—JV

Chapter 14

TAHMIENE MOMTAZI

A FIREBRAND WITH A MISSION

W hen I'm figuring out my blends, I am trying to tell a story," said Maysara winemaker Tahmiene Momtazi. And as I took in the atmosphere at Maysara, it was easy to believe that there were many stories to be told.

Maysara Winery is a 538-acre estate in McMinnville, Oregon. We were seated in a cozy parlor within a forty-thousand-square-foot structure. The space is used for intimate gatherings, such as bridal showers. A massive wooden staircase connected it to a more expansive area.

The stairs were thought provoking in that they were simple, elegant and seemingly ancient yet recently built. Walking down them reminded me of being a small child, as they were so big. Looking across the vast interior space and at its architectural details filled me with awe for its grandeur, but it was not like the Palace of Versailles; it was something lacking pretense. It was a monument, though, but to something holding the earth scared. The structure was built of stone and wood, with 95 percent of the materials harvested from the estate. It was clad in recycled clapboard made from exhausted oak wine barrels that were dismembered and flattened. The structure's vertical columns were made from large peeled tree trunks.

The light color of the oak throughout the room made the vast space bright and welcoming. The most dramatic architectural elements were three Romanesque arches that formed the winery entryway, each having its own massive barn door. They were so large you could fit a small airplane

Wild turkeys roam through Maysara's grapevines. *Maysara Winery.*

The back pond at Maysara Winery buried beneath winter snow. *Maysara Winery.*

through each of them. These arches date back to ancient times, and the configurations allow significant spans to be achieved. This is because all the combined forces can hold them together in a state of equilibrium.

On this late March day, the sun's arrival was a huge, uplifting relief after a wet winter in this land that is essentially a cool rainforest. The long rainy season is the tradeoff of such magnificent natural beauty. Such a grand establishment seems like it could be daunting to the tiny winemaker who practices her craft here. But Tahmiene is not one to be stifled.

"My parents left Iran in 1982 after the fall of the shah. They left everything behind and traveled on a motorcycle, first to Pakistan and then to Spain. My mother was pregnant with me when they left, and I was born later that year in Madrid. Eventually, we made it to the United States, and my father worked very hard and made a successful life. My parents gave up everything to give me an education, a better life and the opportunity to do what I do today in my winery. So I make my wines for them, for the family heritage and customs they gave up. And with each one, I put back another detail of what they left behind."

One might think winemaking an interesting occupation after everything Tahmiene and her family had gone through. And the fact is, it did come as a surprise to nearly everyone in the family. Tahmiene originally set out to become a pediatrician and spent two years as a science major before she succumbed to the allure of winemaking. But she wasn't prepared to share her new plans with her family. So, she secretly changed majors and received a Bachelor of Science degree in new food science and technology in fermentation science from Oregon State University.

"I didn't tell my father I was studying winemaking until I graduated. I was very secretive. I guess that's the Scorpio in me…when I want to shock, I shock. But I think he sensed what I was doing. I think he was actually glad but didn't want to get his hopes up."

Tahmiene's father, Moe, developed a love of winemaking as a child. His father would make wine as a gift to family and friends in celebration of the Zoroastrian New Year, an important holiday that included gatherings and gift giving among close friends, family and colleagues. As a lighthearted aside, he added, "My dad thought it was a sin to sell wine. He would probably turn in his grave to know I sell wine! It is just part of the culture. It is a Zoroastrian thing."

Eventually, the combination of Moe's business success and love of wine would lead him to build Maysara, which paved the way for Tahmiene to

MAYSARA WINERY

Maysara Winery and Momtazi Vineyard are nestled in the foothills of the McMinnville AVA. Being located at the mouth of the Van Duzer corridor, cool marine breezes and different soil types on 532 acres of rolling hills produce an exceptional fruit sought after by many top wineries. The vineyard's efforts from the beginning have been based on having a self-sufficient farm to produce all its needs from within. It is Demeter-certified biodynamic both at the vineyard and winery. This philosophy is carried into its new winery facility being built with native materials supplied by its own estate.

OWNER: *Moe and Flora Momtazi*
WINEMAKER: *Tahmiene Momtazi*
VARIETALS: *Pinot noir, Pinot blanc, Pinot gris, Pinot noir rose*

TASTING ROOM LOCATION:
15765 Southwest Muddy Valley Road, McMinnville, OR, 97128

HOURS: *Monday–Saturday, 12:00 p.m.–5:00 p.m.*
FEE: *$10*
CONTACT: *(503) 843-1234; wine@maysara.com*

VINEYARDS:
- *Momtazi Vineyard (McMinnville AVA)*

become a winemaker. But it's not in her nature to take anything for granted or fail to earn whatever comes her way. So, after graduating from college, she headed to New Zealand to work with Kim Crawford at the Blenheim facility for a year. Then, in 2007, Tahmiene came home to Oregon and accepted the position of winemaker at Maysara.

Maysara Winery is situated on a foothill and connected to civilization by a gravel road alongside neat rows of vines. The estate is surrounded by old-growth oak trees, blackberry bushes and other naturally occurring plants that flavor the estate's wines.

The day I was there, unusual white cows and wild turkeys roamed freely through the "pre-bud-break" vineyards. Their droppings provide fertilizer, and their grazing serves as a natural lawnmower, an energy saver that is also cost effective. A Demeter-certified biodynamic vineyard, Maysara is all about what's natural, and the animals are part of the delicate natural balance that supports a healthy ecosystem.

While sustainability or environmental stewardship is a mainstream way of life in Oregon, the strong natural bent at Maysara is a cultural tradition that reaches back thousands of years to ancient times and fables of highly evolved kingdoms with lesser-known characters than their Greek and Romans counterparts.

In ancient Persia (what is now Iran), the earliest evidence of winemaking comes from 5400 BC. And in the Persian language of Farsi, *mey* is the word for wine, and *saghi* is the wine pourer. Both are central motifs in ancient Persian literature and art. The person who pours the wine is actually more celebrated than the winemaker. That person was a spiritual leader people would go to for wisdom. Thus the name of the winery, Maysara, is a Persian word that means house of wine, but it represents the deeper meaning of the sacred place where wisdom was sought and shared over a glass of mey with the saghi.

Maysara's vineyards cover 250 of its 538 acres in the picturesque McMinnville foothills. Any route that gets you there would make an excellent photo shoot for a scenic picture calendar.

At Maysara, there are at least nine different soil types and rock subsurface, and elevations reach up to 780 feet above sea level. These variables and many others create flavor diversity in Maysara's wines. With age and root depth come even more changes in the character of the fruits and the wine in your glass. Earth and fruit are among the variables, as are climate and surrounding vegetation.

Maysara's vineyard is segmented into "blocks" that are named for fruit type and location, which is typical in the wine industry. The varieties are called "clones." An easy way to think of it is to liken it to gardening. A hydrangea variation at one location would be a different block than the same hydrangea variation at another. Age of the vine, root depth, subtle climate differences in locations, elevation and climate, as well as soil variations, all converge to affect the grapes from each block. In sum, this vineyard is similar to a spice rack, and pinches of this and that fruit are blended to create the wine you drink. Soil composition, climate, temperature variations and seasonal weather and many other variables all play roles in the taste and quality of the harvested grapes.

The Momtazi Vineyard displaying autumn's yellow leaves. *Maysara Winery.*

Maysara's Jamsheed wine is a Pinot noir composed of select fruits harvested throughout the estate vineyards. Explaining her Jamsheed wine, Tahmiene mused, "It is the entire vineyard together. I wanted people to see that."

Jamsheed is the name of a fabled Persian king who could look into his wine chalice and see his entire kingdom. The "fourth king of the world," the Great Jamsheed is credited with the introduction of the solar year and most arts and sciences, as well as the serendipitous invention of wine. There are many variations of this tale, but the version of the story that Moe and Flora knew as Persian kids says that a handful of death-row criminals in the king's dungeon were used as lab rats on what was thought to be "spoiled juice" that was smoking and bubbling. Unbeknownst to all, the "spoilage" was actually the result of fermentation caused by the breakdown of the grapes by yeast into alcohol. The prisoners drank the so-called poison, and it was discovered that the effects were very pleasant and their spirits were lifted. The jail guards took the discovery to Jamsheed, who became so enamored of this new beverage that he decreed that all grapes grown in his kingdom were to be devoted to winemaking. While most wine historians view this story as pure legend, there is archaeological evidence that wine was known and extensively traded by the early Persian kings.

Simply put, Tahmiene's philosophy on winemaking is that if you put the work into closely monitoring and caring for every aspect of your vineyard, you will deduce what is best. "I do what I need to do and develop wines I think are best for the brand. If you want to psych yourself out, you will. But you must relax, and if you do, the wine will also be relaxed."—VP

Chapter 15

STEWART BOEDECKER AND ATHENA PAPPAS

IN PURSUIT OF SOMETHING PERFECT

When sitting alone with Stewart Boedecker and Athena Pappas in their Northwest Portland tasting room, talking about wine and their path to wine, I enjoyed hearing what they had to say, but I believe I was even more taken with the way they said it. First and foremost, Athena and Stewart are in love. And that feeling permeates the conversation.

They're in love not only with each other but also with wine and the idea of wine—with the pursuit of a thing that might be somehow perfect, with the desire to share their journey with each other and with all who wish to step onto the path with them.

At first glance, they appear a misfit couple. Stewart, tall and fair and affable, speaking with all the precision his engineering profession demands. And Athena, small and intuitive and free associating, reflecting the deep spice of her Greek heritage.

But then I notice that they look more at each other than they look at me. They finish each other's sentences. They laugh at stories before they're fully told. They touch each other frequently and with meaning. And they make wine together.

TESTING THE WATER

It was Stewart's idea to get into winemaking. Athena had never given it a thought and wasn't even sure it was a good idea, but Stewart wanted to do it, so she went along for the ride. Stewart had begun cooking as a child, following recipes, pairing flavors and creating food that others enjoyed. Over the years, his love for food never left, and as with many people, good food led him to an appreciation of good wine. But Stewart is a maker at heart, and wine was no different from his other pursuits. He needed to learn how to make the wine he sought.

His big break came in 1996 when he attended a presentation by Eric Hamacher, who would go on to found the Carlton Winemakers Studio. "I met Eric Hamacher back in '96 when I knew a little about winemaking but not a lot. I talked to him after a lecture he gave and told him I wanted to learn more about winemaking, and to my amazement, he said, 'Hey, just come work with me.' And I thought, wow, really? I can learn this for free?"

He continues, "So I set up my schedule where I could go work for Eric until noon and then work kind of a modified swing shift at my Intel job.

Stewart Boedecker explains his winemaking process to winery visitors. *Boedecker Cellars.*

And '96 was like the coldest, rainiest, nastiest vintage, and I still just loved it. There's nothing like walking into a winery in the middle of harvest, and it's packed full of fermenting Pinot noirs. It's just massive sensory overload. That's what hooked me."

And what's Athena take on this? "I had no idea what was coming. None. We were dating when Stewart met Eric, and I was mostly happy about that because it meant that I got my autumns to myself, which I enjoyed. Plus, I went out to the winery when he got started, and I was like, 'Yeah, it's cold and there are bugs.' Not appealing, so I didn't mind not being there."

She adds, "But I understood that if we were going to be together, I needed to learn this. So we took classes together, and we learned more and more about wine, but honestly, I didn't truly understand a damn thing until our own first harvest in 2003. Learning my way around a winery and shaking earwigs out of my hair. Smelling and tasting and hurting and aching and crying. Not crying out of frustration at some boss you have, but crying from sheer exhaustion and knowing that you can't stop and go home because this wine is going to change in the next few hours and how you respond is going to determine whether it goes bad or becomes beautiful. Now I can smell where the wine is going, what stage it's in. I can understand it, and that's pretty amazing."

BUILDING ON A STUDIO START

Athena got her baptism by fire in 2003, but Stewart had been steadily assisting Eric Hamacher since their introduction in '96, including the first year of operation for the Carlton Winemakers Studio in 2002. His dedication helped pave the way for their personal label.

"In 2003, when we started up, that was the year after Eric opened the studio, and he figured out how to wedge us into a little corner there. We made four hundred cases our first year. And there's no way without that place that we could have made wine as good as what we made. Because even though we were only making four hundred cases a year, we had a world-class facility and equipment. It was a fantastic springboard place."

Athena expanded on the value of the studio incubator and how it set them up to build their own winery in the city of Portland. "We finally got big enough around 2007 to leave and go out on our own, so we built this

Boedecker Cellars

Getting to Boedecker Cellars winery and tasting room is not the same type of experience as driving through wine country's vineyards, but it is interesting nonetheless, and it's a shorter trip for Portland residents. Located on the outskirts of the City's Northwest Industrial District, Boedecker Cellars provides an island of friendly refinement in a rough-hewn region of town. It also provides a place to meet two engaging winemakers and sample their outstanding creations.

Year Founded: *2003*
Owners: *Stewart Boedecker and Athena Pappas*
Winemakers: *Stewart Boedecker and Athena Pappas*
Varietals: *Pinot noir, Pinot blanc, Pinot gris, Chardonnay*

Tasting Room Location:
2621 Northwest Thirtieth Avenue, Portland, OR, 97210

Hours:
Saturday and Sunday 1:00 p.m.–5:00 p.m., or midweek by appointment
Fee: *$10*
Contact: *(503) 224-5778; info@boedeckercellars.com*

Sustainability Features:
* *vineyards organically farmed, most LIVE certified*
* *cellar: all ferments are native yeasts*
* *barrels used up to ten or more years*
* *all winemaking is done by hand*

place in 2008 and got moved in here just in time for the 2008 harvest, which is a whole other story. Regardless, when we were going through that process of building a winery, a lot of our setup was based on equipment we had used in Carlton. Because of that experience, we knew exactly what we needed."

Athena Pappas and Stewart Boedecker at work in their urban winery in northwest Portland. *Boedecker Cellars.*

Regardless of the process, the challenges or anything else, now that Stewart and Athena have their own winery and are able, year after year, to make their own wine, they are happy. And there's no doubt that the popularity of their wines has contributed to their sense of well-being.

Stewart explains how he feels. "I just love it. Making Oregon pinot… every year is different because the climate's so close to the edge. But it's this huge puzzle you get every year. What do you do in the vineyard? How do you respond to the weather? When do you pick each little section? How do you handle the fermenters? And how do you put the final blend together? It satisfies these great intellectual and tactile needs I have all at the same time."

Athena expands, "And after you figure out those puzzle pieces, you're still trying to guide it. To have a wine sit in bottle for five years, seven years, and watch it change and still be appealing is like the end-all, be-all. So you still have to have a sense of where it's going to go. That's the experience part of it, which I'm getting better at."

CREATING A STYLE

As she looks back at her winemaking history, it surprises Athena that the physical aspects of winemaking first won her over. But she believes that the intuitive and intellectual qualities of the work continue to pull her in. "It's like what Stewart said…how it's 'of the senses.' You're aware of everything. The smells. Everything. But it's not just manual labor. It's intellectual. And there's so much instinct and reaction going on."

Stewart agrees. "And that instinct-reaction piece is so important. Everybody I know who makes good Oregon Pinot, everybody's technically competent. Nobody just outright blows their wine because they don't know what they're doing. But there are some people who not only are technically very savvy but also have that touch and feel piece. The people who have that special touch, who feel what needs to happen with the wine at any particular time, who pay attention to the extra level of detail and follow their gut reaction…that's when you get the extra expanse around the style, the extra layers, the bright bits of roughness around the edges."

Stewart and Athena are the embodiment of detail and intuition, but interestingly, the styles of the wine each of them make are different. When Stewart describes his wine, he uses words like "precise," "pure" and "delicate." Athena looks for something primal that she can just react to. She explains, "We have our own representations of all our hard work. Stewart's wine is just very bright…that pure fruit gets you in the very beginning, and it's very pretty in the mid-palate. Mine is like…wait for it, and then *boom*, and it kind of stays with you for a while."

Stewart Boedecker ponders a sample of Pinot noir. *Boedecker Cellars*.

She concludes, "But that said, this is Pinot, which is lighter and layered. So what I love are the aromatics. You smell the Pinot…the fruit, the dirt, whatever spices are there. I get frustrated because there are only so many descriptors, and I'm limited to like five words to explain what it is exactly that gives me goose bumps, but it's something darker with more *oomph*."

Bright or dark, it's clear that Athena and Stewart love their wine, almost as much as they love working together to make it.—JV

Chapter 16

DON CRANK III

I CAN'T BE CRAZY ANYMORE

If you can envision a heated debate over blending in a vast wine cellar where Frank Zappa or some hard rock or free jazz is blaring, pranking is common and the workday is intensely long, you get the vibe at Willamette Valley Vineyards and Don Crank's life as head winemaker.

In January 2012, at age thirty-five, Don Crank took over the helm of winemaking at Willamette Valley Vineyard, a Turner, Oregon winery that encompasses 320 planted acres and distributes up to 120,000 cases of wine annually.

It was a promotion to oversee a staff of up to fifty-five employees during harvest and as many as thirty wine labels, half of them his favorite varietal, Pinot noir. Alas, it was a time of mixed emotions as he was taking over for his mentor, his friend, the man who gave him the rare opportunity to join a winemaking team, to learn and eventually take part in every aspect of winemaking. Since 2003, Don played the role of the scientific sidekick to the winemaker who first interviewed him: the award-winning Forrest Klaffke, whom the vineyard owner lovingly titled "Winemaker Extraordinaire."

Forrest was a mix between a Willy Wonka and a Charles Eames. He had a wild, welcoming gleam in his eye that just said that anything *is* possible. He passed away at Christmastime in 2011 after a three-year battle with cancer that ended his twenty-nine-year career. He was fifty-six years old.

I met Forrest and Don selling wine barrels. Unbeknownst to me, Forrest was in the final stages of a life-and-death struggle when I called to set an appointment. I stumbled over the pronunciation of the France-based

Willamette Valley Vineyards' winemaker Don Crank checks early-season vines. *Willamette Valley Vineyards.*

cooperage I was representing in my introductory call. His response was along the lines of "who gives a *expletive*. Come on down."

I learned of Forrest's illness and his passing during a follow-up sales call the week before his memorial. I was compelled to attend. Forrest's memorial on January 15, 2012, was one poetic tribute after another. He was a hardworking, fun, funny guy. Klaffke made a decision to die sooner and forego cancer treatments in order to avoid the mentally debilitating aspects of chemotherapy; he wanted to use Q4 2011 to prepare the historical blending records for the years ahead. Klaffke had to see everything through, according to his numerous memorial presenters, which included Don and Forrest's eldest child: Don's newly installed assistant winemaker, Daniel Shepherd, the former self-described "cellar rat."

Willamette Valley Vineyard is a flat organization where winemaking is a team sport, long hours are the norm and multitasking is required, as is expertise across winemaking disciplines. "Forrest would not ask you to do anything he would not do himself," said Don, who follows Forrest's leadership

WILLAMETTE VALLEY VINEYARDS

Willamette Valley Vineyards has been producing high-quality, sustainably grown Pinot noir and other cool-climate varieties for more than twenty-eight years—earning the distinction as "One of America's Great Pinot Noir Producers" by Wine Enthusiast Magazine. *The mission at WVV is to create elegant, classic Oregon wines from the Willamette Valley Appellation while serving as stewards of the land. Founder Jim Bernau believes we are rewarded with wines that taste better when made from naturally grown wine grapes. Tending the vines by hand and using minimalist winemaking techniques in small-batch fermentations, Bernau and his people strive to capture the unique sense of place that comes from their vineyard soils. Willamette Valley Vineyards was the first to use natural cork in its bottles certified by the Rainforest Alliance to Forest Stewardship Council standards and offers ten cents for any wine bottle returned to its tasting room for recycling. To reduce carbon footprint, all company tractors and delivery vehicles run on biofuel, and the vineyard offers up to fifty gallons a month free to employees for commuting to work. Willamette Valley Vineyards wines have been served at the White House and the James Beard House, and they are available at some of the finest restaurants and wine shops throughout the world.*

OWNER: *Jim Bernau*
WINEMAKER: *Don Crank III*
VARIETALS: *Pinot noir, Pinot gris, Chardonnay, Riesling*

TASTING ROOM LOCATION:
8800 Southeast Enchanted Way, Turner, OR, 97392

HOURS: *open daily, 11:00 a.m.–6:00 p.m.*
FEE: *$5 and $10*
CONTACT: *(503) 588-9463; info@wvv.com*

VINEYARDS:
- *WVV Estate in Turner (Willamette Valley AVA)*
- *Elton Vineyard (Eola-Amity Hills AVA)*
- *Tualatin Estate (Willamette Valley AVA)*

A stunning view of the Willamette Valley from Willamette Valley Vineyards. *Willamette Valley Vineyards.*

style. For example, the team works an average of 13.5-hour days during harvest. Off-season, Don finds himself on the road, joining sales people on calls or at winemaker dinners, interacting with wine enthusiasts and wine experts of all kinds. "It is a busy life. Forrest and I split up the stuff," said Don, adding that it has been really busy since Forrest's passing. "Daniel is here and is doing quite good at it."

Daniel is a bilingual, supercharged multitasker, a "Karate Kid" according to Don. "He's [directing the] unloading of a truck in two languages and at the same time running an earth filter. Every good winemaker I've ever met has a lot of things to do at once. You have to do a lot at once and prioritize things. The master was Forrest Klaffke. He would stuff this place full of logistics."

At Willamette Valley Vineyards, the winemaking philosophy is make a balanced wine that showcases the widely varying vineyard harvests and not to force a strategy on the grapes but rather identify and embrace what the year brings. "It's a hippy thing to say, but pay attention to what the grapes want to do," said Don. "Oregon wines are more vintage dependent. We have wide and wild swings in the character of the wines, and the huge upside is good, amazingly good, wines. How rare and hard it is to make. We have philosophical discussions about it, such as if there were no evil in the world, what then?"

To Don, winemaking is similar to being a chef with "no fire and dinner takes a year and a half to make." He added that it requires a good memory so you can compare years (or vintages) and know what you are looking for in the next.

Growing up in Memphis, Tennessee, playing *Dungeons & Dragons*, the first time Don "got drunk was off the wine I made myself." He was sixteen years old and thought that it would be fun to buy a mail-order winemaking kit.

Don's love of fermentation followed him through college. He was an important asset on campus since he made beer for parties. He majored in biochemistry at Purdue, and after receiving his Bachelor of Science degree, he enrolled in another undergraduate program in food science. Three credits away from graduation, he dropped out to sell cars—Saturns, to be specific. "I thought this is what you will be doing in real life, and I don't want to do this at all; my father stopped funding me after that," Don said.

Don is the son of a soy protein chemist and the oldest of four boys. He is dyslexic, and his attachment to numbers is so strong that they evoke emotions in him. Alternatively, Don has tremendous trouble with spelling and remembering names, especially complicated ones. As a result, he had to develop puzzle-solving skills to compensate. His "fastidious attention to digits" allows him to perform algorithms in his head. In truth, his dyslexia created strengths that made him an important asset on Willamette Valley Vineyards' collaborative winemaking team. "Filtering through the minutia lends itself to seeing the wine from the Gestalt of it all together," he said. "You don't have to be like that to make great wine," Don said. "You are only as strong as your team."

Don's career choice was solidified in 1999. At that time, his father offered to fund an adventure to any destination in the world. It was something Don's father would do for all four of his sons and a Crank family tradition. Don picked the internationally acclaimed Burgundy wine region in France, and he went to volunteer at a vineyard during harvest. He returned with a career choice in winemaking. And he came to Oregon because he believed the Willamette Valley to be the best American answer to Burgundy's wine region, especially for Pinot noir. Both are in the 45th parallel, the geographic area known as the ideal climate for wine growing as it provides the perfect balance of temperature, humidity and soil.

The late Forrest Klaffke, former Willamette Valley Vineyards winemaker, reflects in the winery doorway. *Willamette Valley Vineyards.*

With this in mind, Don Crank set out for Oregon in his grandma's hand-me-down Lincoln Continental. The old gas guzzler got him here, and he "couch-surfed," waited tables and worked as a laborer at another winery, where he was remanded to intensive labor such as cleaning tanks for ten hours a day with, in Don's words, no hope of climbing the ranks. "It was more like, 'Here's some wine, thank you very much.'" Don eventually met Noel Arce, at that time a brewer. Noel hired Don and would later leave the brewery for a winemaking post and eventually land at Willamette Valley Vineyards.

On Noel's good recommendation in 2003, Don got in front of Forrest. "I came in and laid on him all this biochemistry jargon," Don said. He thought he had blown the interview. He was a biochemist by training, but he had everything to learn about winemaking.

Biochemists are typically remanded to the lab, but Forrest hired him as part of the winemaking team despite his lack of experience. He challenged Don way beyond his comfort zone immediately, assigning Don to the finicky bottling machine, a difficult machine that is certain to break down for even a mechanically adept person. "I have good ideas now on how to fix the thing; it always involves a big hammer," Don said.

It was 2004 when Forrest eventually began to take Don's advice on blends. "Forrest and I fought like cats and dogs," Don said. "We are both strong-willed. I'm the oldest of four boys, and he's the youngest of eight kids. A lot of good ideas came out of that fighting."

We were seated in the winemakers' cellar office. It was a jumble of test tubes, things that spin them, paperwork and an assortment of wall hangings, including Don's Bachelor of Science degree from Purdue University. Daniel was there, too. He looked up to say to Don, "You're a nerdy guy, and we kind of pick on you. It's the only upper hand we have."

With the change in command, Don's role has changed as well. "I'm the boss, and I can't be shot down; I can't be crazy anymore," Don said, adding that now he's looking to Shepherd to play that outer-edge, idea-man role.—VP

Epilogue

IN MEMORIAM

FORREST GLENN KLAFFKE, 1955–2011

Willamette Valley Vineyards winemaker extraordinaire Forrest Glenn Klaffke passed away on December 26, 2011, after a three-year battle with cancer. Over the course of his thirty-four-year winemaking career, the fifty-six-year-old collaborative winemaker became known for his award-winning Pinot noirs. He passed away at home, surrounded by his family.

Forrest began his winemaking career in California, screening wine grapes for quality at Bonded Winery No. 7, a United Vintners concern near Sacramento. He further refined his skills working in Robert Mondavi's cellar, where his hard work and dedication earned him the promotion to cellar foreman, supervising a crew of forty at Sebastiani.

Unsatisfied with California's Pinot noir and excited about the potential for Pinot noir in Oregon, Forrest accepted an offer to join the winemaking staff at Willamette Valley Vineyards to make small, hand-crafted lots of Pinot noir. Four days after their wedding, Forrest and his new wife, Maria, made the trek to Oregon.

Willamette Valley Vineyards founder Jim Bernau and Forrest shared a vision and philosophy of what they wanted their Pinot noir to be. Over nineteen years with Willamette Valley Vineyards, Forrest rose from cellar master to assistant winemaker. In 2002, he was named head winemaker. Creating an array of 90-plus-point wines, including the acclaimed 94-point 2008 O'Brien Pinot Noir, his thirty years of dedication and focus earned him the distinction from friends and colleagues as "Winemaker Extraordinaire."

Forrest was further acknowledged by *Wine & Spirits* magazine, which named the winery one of its 2011 "Top 100 Wineries of the World."

Forrest had a tremendous work ethic, being the first to arrive at the winery each day and often the last to leave. His approach to his work was uncompromising, leading to the high quality and acclaim for which his wines are known. His approach to blending was collaborative; he included his winemaking team and fellow winery colleagues by soliciting their opinions. Forrest was the sort of person who would rather share a sense of collective ownership in the final product. He felt that this was the best way to do the very best.

During his three-year battle with cancer, Forrest decided to share his office with winemaker Don Crank, to collaborate on each lot and blend and to train Don for the time when Forrest would no longer be able to work. Knowing that he was losing his fight with his illness, Forrest chose to stay with the winemaking team through the challenging 2011 harvest, forgoing chemotherapy treatments to keep his mind clear for managing the fermenters.

Forrest was born in Lodi, California, the son of Waldon and Pauline Mary (Clow) Klaffke. On April 15, 1993, Forrest married Maria Vatsula in Stockton, California. Forrest is survived by his wife; by his children, Daniel David Shepherd and his wife, Rachel Shepherd, of Salem, and Georgianna Mikala Klaffke of Jefferson; and by his brothers, Ralph Klaffke of New Zealand, Richard Klaffke of Astoria and Kurt Klaffke of Neahkahnie. Forrest's first grandchild and Daniel's first child, Layla Marie Shepherd, was born on August 24, 2012.

APPENDIX

Courtesy of the Willamette Valley Wineries Association.

Northern Willamette Valley: The Road Less Traveled

From Portland, head west on Highway 26 and connect through the back roads to Highway 47, enjoying the lovely views and wines in Portland's backyard. If you keep heading south, your wine tasting stamina (and designated driver) will lead you through the wineries of Forest Grove, Hillsboro, Gaston, Yamhill, Carlton and beyond.

Southern Willamette Valley: Southern Sipping

The perfect route for the adventurous wine taster seeking some of the valley's most distinct wines. From the north, it's a short drive down I-5 to Salem and west to 99W, where you can get off the beaten path and visit the many wineries near Albany, Corvallis, Monmouth, Monroe and surrounding areas. You will be thankful you came!

Eola-Amity Hills: Head for the Hills!

Experience the back road charm of Eola-Amity Hills wineries outside Salem. This hidden gem is only forty-five minutes from Portland. Head south on I-5 and then west to these small, family-owned wineries near Salem. For an unforgettable entrance into wine country, take your friends and family across the Wheatland Ferry.

The Back Door to Dundee Hills and Chehalem Mountains

When it comes to wine tasting, we all want to spend more time visiting our favorite wineries and less time on the road. Avoid traffic and enjoy the ride with this back road route: in Newberg, take Springbrook to Zimri and then turn left onto North Valley Road. Take Dopp Road to 240 and turn left on Worden Hill Road, which winds all the way up and down the hills to Dundee.

Road to Carlton and McMinnville: Urban and Rural Escape

Carlton and McMinnville offer a unique wine tasting experience: tasting rooms pouring world class wines all within a walk around the block (or two). Enjoy the scenic back roads of Highway 240 out of Newberg to Kuehne Road into Carlton and then back to Highway 99 into McMinnville. Can't make it to all of your favorite wineries in one day? Make this the perfect two-day urban and rural escape.

WINERIES BY TOWN

Membership listing courtesy of the Willamette Valley Wineries Association.

Amity

Amity
Brooks
Coelho
Dukes Family
Iota

Beaverton

Cooper Mountain
Ponzi

Carlton

Andrew Rich
Angela Estate
Angel Vine
Anne Amie
Belle Pente
Cana's Feast
Carlton Cellars
Carlton Winemakers
  Studio
Ghost Hill
Hamacher
K&M
Kramer
Lachini
Laurel Ridge
Lemelson
Merriman
Monks Gate
Omero
Retour
Scott Paul
Seven of Hearts
Siltstone
Soter
Wahle
Wildaire

Cornelius

Árdíri
A Blooming Hill

Corvallis

Tyee

Dallas

Amalie Robert
Illahe
Namasté
Van Duzer

Dayton

Archery Summit
Armonéa
De Ponte
Domaine Drouhin
  Oregon
Domaine Serene
Durant
Methven
Seufert
Stoller
Vista Hills
White Rose
Winter's Hill

Dundee

Antica Terra	Domaine Trouvere	Lange
Argyle	Duck Pond	Le Cadeau
Ayoub	Dusky Goose	Sokol Blossser
Bella Vida	Erath	Thistle
Black Walnut	Four Graces	Torii Mor
Crumbled Rock	Hawkins	Willful Wine
Dobbes	Hyland Estates	Winderlea

Eugene

Sweet Cheeks

Forest Grove

Apolloni
David Hill
Montinore

Gaston

Adea	Harper Voit	Rocky Point
Big Table Farm	Kramer	Tendril
Cornerstone Oregon	Patton Valley	
Elk Cove	Plum Hill	

Hillsboro

Freja
J. Albin

Independence

Redgate

McMinnville

Anthony Dell	Eyrie	R. Stuart	
Biggio Hamina	Matello	Terra Vina	Yamhill Valley
Coeur de Terre	Maysara	Twelve	Vineyards
Coleman	Panther Creek	Walnut City	Youngberg Hill
Dominio IV	Remy	Westrey	Z'IVO

Molalla

Alexeli

Monmouth

Airlie

Monroe

Benton-Lane
Broadley
Ebony

Newberg

Adelsheim
Alexana
Anam Cara
Anderson Family
Aramenta
Arborbrook
August
Ayres
Beaux Frères
Bergström
Brick House
Chehalem
Colene Clemens

Et Fille
Fox Farm
Hip Chicks
J.K. Carriere
Lachini
Longplay
Natalie's Estate
Owen Roe
Patricia Green
Penner-Ash
Privé
Purple Hands
Raptor Ridge

Redman
REX HILL
Roco
Shea
Sineann
Styring
Tresori
Trisaetum
Utopia
Vidon
VX (Vercingetorix)

Portland

Boedecker
Hip Chicks
Island Mana

Rickreall

Cherry Hill
Johan
Left Coast

Salem

Arcane Cellars
Bethel Heights
Bryn Mawr
Cristom
Cubanisimo
Evening Land

Evesham Wood
Honeywood
Mahonia
Redhawk
Stangeland
St. Innocent

Vitae Springs
Walter Scott
Whistling Dog
Witness Tree

Sheridan

J Wrigley

Sherwood

Alloro   Et Fille
Beckham   Ponzi
Blakeslee   Quailhurst
Hawks View

Troutdale

Edgefield
(McMenamins)

Tualatin

Union Wine

Wilsonville

Carabella
Terra Vina

Yamhill

Atticus
Lenné
Saffron Fields
Soléna
Stag Hollow
WillaKenzie

INDEX

ABOUT THE AUTHORS
AND ILLUSTRATOR

VIVIAN PERRY is a marketer and former New York City features writer who put her roots down in Oregon fifteen years ago. Raised in Franklin Lakes, New Jersey, she spent most of the 1990s as a staff writer for the *Staten Island Advance*. Her journalism awards include a trophy from the New York City Chapter of the Society of Professional Journalists. Her winning story was about two orphaned New York City teenagers who faced eviction from a public housing complex over a survivorship technicality. A massive public outcry resulted from the story. As a result, the city granted the two teens survivor rights to their deceased grandmother's home, thus allowing them to remain and return to college and finish high school with a roof over their

heads. Vivian holds a Bachelor of Arts degree in print journalism from New York University. In recent years, Vivian has served on the board of the Oregon Chapter of the Society of Marketing Professional Services. She received the chapter's 2009 President's Award and was named a finalist in the the *Daily Journal of Commerce*'s 2008 Rainmaker competition. Visit her on the Web at http://salonpdx.blogspot.com.

JOHN VINCENT lives and works in Portland, Oregon, but he plays throughout the Pacific Northwest. He prefers drinking Pinot noir when he's winding down a writing session; craft beer when he's talking with friends, acquaintances and complete strangers; and kombucha when he's pretending to be a healthy, well-balanced person. He feels like he owes his writing career, modest though it may be, to his lifelong desire to avoid real work; the thoughtful and loving support of his wife, Lisa Holmes; and the city of Portland, which provides a culture of belief and inspires the courage to live your dreams. John studied creative writing at the University of Kansas. His writing awards include first place in the Carruth Memorial Poetry Competition (University of Kansas), second place in the Kay Snow Writing Contest—Poetry and third place in the Kay Snow Writing Contest—Screenwriting. His collection of poetry, *Repairing Shattered Glass*, is available on Amazon.com.

SARAH SCHLESINGER is a New Jersey native, born in Bergen County and raised in Sussex County. At an early age, she won the New Jersey Governor's Award for Visual Arts and then went on to attend Pratt at Munson-Williams-Proctor and Pratt Institute Brooklyn, where she majored in drawing. In 2008, she graduated with high honors at the top of her class. Since graduating, she has kept busy with her own creative endeavors and participated in two shows in Williamsburg, one of which was primarily a solo exhibition at 8 of Swords, a tattoo and art gallery space. She's had several jobs in the art field and now works part time at a children's clothing company in addition to a high-end ceramic production studio. She also does freelance illustration and graphic work, mainly for independent films, book projects and small local businesses. She lives and works in Brooklyn, New York. You can see her artwork at www.sarahschlesingerart.com.